CONTENTS

Eat Smart Eat Raw

by Kate Wood

SQUAREONE
PUBLISHERS

COVER DESIGNERS: Phaedra Mastrocola and Jeannie Tudor
FRONT COVER PHOTO: Getty Images, Inc.
BACK COVER PHOTOS: Michelle Garrett
INTERIOR ART: Jeannie Tudor
IN-HOUSE EDITOR: Ariel Colletti
TYPESETTER: Theresa Wiscovitch

Square One Publishers
115 Herricks Road
Garden City Park, NY 11040
(516) 535-2010 • (877) 900-BOOK
www.squareonepublishers.com

Library of Congress Cataloging-in-Publication Data

Wood, Kate.
    Eat smart eat raw / Kate Wood.
       p. cm.
    Includes index.
    ISBN 0-7570-0261-7 (pbk.)
    1. Cookery (Natural foods) 2. Raw foods. I. Title.
    TX741.W65 2006
    641.5'63--dc22

                                                2005033236

Reprinted under special arrangement with Grub Street, London, England, UK

Text Copyright © 2006 by Kate Wood
Photo Copyright © 2006 by Grub Street

Printed in the United States of America

10   9   8   7   6   5   4   3   2   1

To my boys—
Chris, Reuben, Ethan and Zachary

ACKNOWLEDGMENTS

I am deeply grateful to everyone who has accompanied me along my raw journey. Especially to Nikki, for being my first raw sister. To Ysanne, the amazing organic rock goddess. To Jill, Holly, Tish and Shazzie for keeping it real in the UK. To Shazzie again for turning me onto so many amazing superfoods which have profoundly changed my experience of life. To my raw Brighton family, Gela, Cathie, Sue, and Joel. To all the people who have given Raw Living their energy and love, especially Sara, James and family, and Andy and crew. And most importantly to Chris, Reuben, Ethan and Zachary, without whom this book would never have happened.

Finally, I wish to acknowledge the profound magic of the higher forces at work in our lives, and the role they have taken in nurturing me, guiding me and leading me to ever more wonderful places.

FOREWORD

You have this book in your hands and you're able to read it. You are so blessed, lucky and abundant. You're in a better position than most other humans on this planet, and I'm so happy that you're choosing to create a beautiful life for yourself and loved ones by appreciating the possibilities that lie before you.

The world of living foods is based upon cutting edge information, yet it's the oldest diet in the world. Yes, you read it right, the raw food diet is not a new fad as some folks may wish you to believe! Before fire, man ate raw, and man was strong! In fact, even now, over 99% of creatures on this planet eat only raw foods. Humans are the odd ones out—and with modern-day farming methods, toxins and nutrient-deficient foods, we're becoming even odder! When one in four people can't conceive naturally, when more people in the world are clinically obese than are starving, when prisons are overflowing, when teenagers are fed apathy and media lies with their burgers and fries, and when everyone knows someone with cancer, don't you think it's great that right now, you are actually making the connection between these problems and the food that people are eating on a daily (sometimes hourly!) basis?

I'm astounded that the phrase "you are what you eat" is so well known, yet so conveniently ignored! While the wild, strong, beautiful and serene animals continue to eat the food they were designed to eat, humans continue to eat anything that they can, whether it's designed to be eaten by them or not (and whether it's actually food or not!).

I have raw food to thank for giving me back my health, happiness and joyous soul. For me, life before raw food was like living in a dark tunnel, and not even seeing the light at the end of it. Life with raw food causes greatness, love, happiness and beautiful reality to constantly show up. There is no comparison between living a cooked (abnormal, man-made) life and a raw (normal and natural) life. Having been on the raw food path since 2000 (and vegan since 1987), I can let you know that we are literally fed lies by the medical profession and nutritionists about what health and healthy food is. We are often told that bread, rice and potatoes are necessary for good health! It's interesting how people fail to thrive, become deficient and can't reach their full potential while these foods are the staples of their diet. I used to feel awful after eating these cooked starch monsters! I'd feel puffiness, weakness, bloatedness, itchiness and tiredness. There were so many "nesses" flying around that they'd pin me down on the couch for a whole night, and I could only manage to reach for the remote control! When I researched raw food, and started eating that way, all my "nesses" disappeared and these cute little "fuls" knocked on the door wanting to come and stay. I warmly welcomed healthful, beautiful, joyful and blissful, and they're still with me six years on!

Thankfully, I'm not the only one to be affected by the raw food revolution, as it is gathering momentum every day! Increasing amounts of people are waking up to the fact that if they want to continue waking up, they need to make radical changes to their lives. Often, the biggest shift to make is in food they eat, simply because it's such a frequent activity. It's great that people now want to vary their diets, try new tastes and introduce these to their children, our future. And all this has been made so easy and fun with *Eat Smart, Eat Raw* as Kate's gentle and reassuring words guide you on your voyage. There are days, weeks and months of recipes here, so just get more and more excited as you try Kate's creations. Raw food cuisine pushes the boundaries of creativity, and Kate's cuisine shows this off wonderfully, simply and consistently. Her recipes and her style are pure joy, created from the heart.

Speaking of the heart, the heart chakra is green—the color of healing. I believe that most of the food we eat should be green, because of its alkalizing, mineralizing, strengthening and love-enhancing capabilities. Most of us don't eat enough green food, and most people have a lot of pain and sadness in their lives. Green food can change this and the juicing and salad recipes in here will guide you!

The book that you're holding is a wonder. It contains real advice and real, workable recipes. I know because I've tried (and enjoyed) many of them! Every now and then, I'll read an article about raw food, and a recipe is mentioned. It's often one of Kate's: Reuben's Dip, Curried Spinach or Sunflower Sausages, for example. This is the great news about Kate's book; it's slowly and steadily pervading the world through its many foreign editions.

On a personal note, I'd heard about this raw food author and mother, Kate Wood, for a few years before I met her. I was always impressed by the way she seemed to manage bringing her children up on such a great diet. When we finally met each other, we spent the day enjoying a good old chat as if we were long-lost friends. Even now, we're in almost daily contact, supporting and nurturing each other in our personal and business lives. In Kate, I see a caring, compassionate, gentle, heart-led and witty soul. Her light shines softly yet persistently on all that she comes into contact with. There's something so unassuming about Kate that makes her believable. There's no hype or self-grandiosity—just a loving woman going about her business in a really mellow way.

It was no surprise to me that she recently convinced many of the mothers at her local Steiner school to become regular users of the superfoods that we both enjoy! Her logic was simple: if you have children to run around after, you can't afford to be tired all the time. Raw food, superfoods and juices supercharge you with energy and vitality. As an added bonus, it's also great that your children see you being so good to yourself because they learn by your example.

There were barely any raw food books a few years ago, and now there is an abundance of them. Raw food cuisine is here to stay. If you're interested in extracting the most from your life, realizing your full potential, feeling more connected to the source, losing your nesses and finding your "fuls," then adding several of Kate's recipes into your weekly food plan is a great place to start. In addition, bringing your children up with lots of fresh raw and organic food will alter the shape of this planet's future. Cooked food weakens the mind, spirit and the body, whereas raw food strengthens them. Raw food such as Kate's cuisine, your life and the planet's health are all linked. They are all one, because everything is all one. Let's all together make an oath to start doing the best for ourselves, because we deserve it. By eating more raw food, you're being your own best friend. You're loving yourself into wellness and happiness.

With love and gratitude,
Shazzie
Author of *Naked Chocolate,*
Detox Your World, Detox Delights and
Managing Director of Rawcreation Ltd

INTRODUCTION

MY STORY

I first embarked on a raw food diet over a decade ago. I had found myself instinctively wanting to eat a lot of fruit and salads, and had heard from friends how health-giving an all-raw diet could be. As the kitchen of the house I was staying in was out of action for three months while it was being renovated, I decided to try it for myself. I took the plunge, and lived on fruit all day, with a big salad and Essene bread and tahini for dinner (neither Essene bread nor tahini are strictly raw, but I didn't know that then). By the time the kitchen was back in order, I was hooked on my new diet, and have stuck with it ever since. Of course, I have had my ups and downs—it is a huge challenge to stick to 100-percent raw, 100 percent of the time. Raw fooders often talk in percentages, claiming to be "70-percent raw" or "90-percent raw" but just to achieve 50 percent long term can make a vast difference in your life.

Although I was convinced of the health benefits, and had experienced for myself how much better I felt, at first the idea that I would stop eating cooked foods altogether was too much, and I would binge on cookies and chips. But gradually, my body came to recognize these as the poisons they truly are. However much I would think that I loved a cooked treat, even one as harmless as apple crumble, when I indulged I would be disappointed, as the cooked dishes came to taste lifeless and dull to me. My body was adjusting to the new levels of energy and the sense of liberation that raw foods gave me, and cooked foods left me on a downer. I began to realize that of course I *could eat* whatever I wanted—but what I really wanted was to feel good all the time. The cleaner my system, the more cooked foods left me with a "hangover:" feeling sluggish and irritable. Gradually, the redundancy of cooking food became a reality to me, and the desire to eat it slipped away completely. Anyone who has become a vegetarian, given up smoking, or overcome any addiction in his or her life, will understand that feeling of a part of your daily living becoming an anathema.

Personally, I had experienced a very rocky relationship with food. Some people say that raw food diets encourage or even create eating disorders; for me it was the reverse, as discovering

1

raw foods helped me to overcome my problems with food. Since adolescence I had been trapped in a binge-fast cycle, leading to periods of emaciation, and periods of being overweight. I believe this was due in part to my instinctive recognition that the foods I was eating weren't right for me: I would reject them, only to be overcome eventually by hunger and greed, which would then be followed by repulsion at all the rubbish I had in my body. Raw foods were a revelation: at last I could eat as much as I wanted, and not feel terrible. Eating half a dozen cookies made me feel sick and tired; eating half a dozen apples left me feeling overfull, but not ill. Over time, as my body got used to being fed, nurtured, and respected, the desire to overeat slipped away. As food no longer disturbed my internal balance, my fear of it disappeared.

Now I am astounded at how little I need to eat. I rarely feel ravenously hungry, and am satiated after relatively small portions of food. Because on a raw diet all our foods are nutrient-dense, the body's requirements are met quickly and efficiently. This in turn means that the body needs less energy for digestion, fighting toxins, and excreting poisons, so it is much less demanding in its requirements. If you want to lose weight then stop counting calories and start counting nutrients! Over-eating happens when the body is searching for nutrients—the brain is waiting for the signal to say that the body has what it needs, and it never comes, so you keep ploughing your way through that packet of cookies, unconsciously looking for the vitamins and minerals you will not find there. In addition, I used to find it very difficult to wake up in the mornings, and needed eight or ten hours of sleep a night or else I felt terrible. Now, because my body is working more efficiently, I

don't wake up feeling fuzzy, but fresh, alert, and ready to go.

When I adopted the raw food diet, I found, in common with many others, changes happening on all levels of my life. Primarily, I experienced a great leap in energy levels: my body was no longer expending such huge amounts of energy on digestion, and so I felt an almost immediate improvement in my vitality. Also quickly apparent was a greater mental clarity and focus. I felt sharper, more alert, and after a long time on the diet I am really conscious of having the resources to be constantly on the go without flagging. Along with these more obvious changes, I also became aware of changes on a deeper level; I am now much happier and lighter, as the positive energy of raw foods fills my being. I am less prone to bad moods and depression, and more satisfied and content. I have a greater tolerance of difficult people and situations, but at the same time know better where my boundaries lie, and what I am prepared to put up with. I notice things in nature that I never did before: the trees look more green and alive, and the changing of the seasons is more apparent to me. All these elements combine to increase hugely my zest for living, leading to a more positive and productive lifestyle. Because I am eating food that is pure and undamaged, I feel whole—more at one with myself and the world around me.

Over the years, I've experienced all the different angles on being raw. At the start, I dived straight in at the deep end, 100-percent raw, including a two-week apple fast just before one Christmas. Then Christmas came, and I went 100-percent cooked! After a few months I stabilized at about 50 percent, then gradually built it up over the next few years until I was 100 percent again. In the following year I did nine months on fruit only, which was amazing at first, but difficult to sustain. At the end of that year, I found out I was pregnant and it was back down to 50 percent again, gradually building back up to 90 percent where I am now, and I've never felt healthier. I have a fruit juice in the morning and a vegetable juice early evening. We have very little cooked food in the house—when I do eat cooked it tends to be on social occasions, if someone has made something specially, or borderline foods such as dried fruits. I cycle everywhere I can, do yoga every day, and swim once a week. I try to eat mainly between the hours of midday and 5:00 P.M. The body has natural cycles. Midday – 8:00 P.M. is the digestion cycle, 8:00 P.M. – 4:00 A.M. is absorption, and 4:00 A.M. – midday is elimination. When you eat during the absorption and elimination cycles, you are going against the body's natural rhythm. For this reason, we have a light breakfast, and an early dinner.

Many leading raw foodists advocate 100-percent raw as the only way to go, but I believe this is too difficult for most people. Undoubtedly, the benefits of being 100-percent raw are huge, but we live in a world where we are constantly coming into contact with cooked foods, and to refuse them continually is both challenging and awkward. I believe it is as important to have a healthy mind as it is to have a healthy body, and the constant denial of other foods can be more harmful than the foods themselves. If you can maintain just 50-percent raw, you will experience a huge increase in your wellbeing. Try eating a side serving of raw food with every meal at first. Then when you are used to this, gradually increase the size of the raw portion to the cooked portion, until you have reached a level that you feel comfortable with (many people find this is around 70 percent).

There are so many borderline foods (nuts, dried fruits, olives, seasonings, and dehydrated goodies), that are not strictly raw, it is difficult to be completely sure about what you are eating. Ultimately, so long as you are eating a diet of fresh, organic wholefoods, with fruit and vegetables as the main elements in your diet, you can't go far wrong. One word of warning, however: it is not uncommon for raw foodists to have trouble with their teeth. Fruit acids destroy the tooth enamel and cause decay. Fresh fruit is not too damaging, but the concentrated sugars in dried fruits and juices can cause problems. If you are worried about your teeth, avoid "grazing" (snacking throughout the day) and clean your teeth half an hour after every meal.

Naturally, most of us are unable to incorporate such huge changes into our lifestyle overnight. On a physical level it isn't hard to do, but food carries deep emotional resonance, and for most of us it is these ties that are difficult to break. Initially, we can be faced by feelings of alienation from our peers, and the sense of missing out on things. But, through perseverance, these feelings fade, and we are left with a vitality and youthfulness that more than make up for anything we may be missing. I still go to restaurants frequently; I usually phone the day before, and state my requirement for a raw vegan salad as my main course. Friends and family may be suspicious at first, but when they see how well you are doing, they may even take on board some of the philosophy themselves. When I eat at other people's houses, it's much easier for them to prepare some fresh fruit and vegetables, than to cater for any other way of eating; it's equally easy for me to bring a dish myself. If you approach the diet with a positive attitude, others will too; if they see you being guarded and awkward, they are more likely to start interrogating you. If the subject comes up in general conversation, I just say that I am a vegan. If people are genuinely interested, then I love to talk about raw foods, but I have learned from experience that if people are not ready to entertain the concept, it is best left alone altogether.

I believe that raw fooders will become more and more accepted over the next few decades, to the same degree that vegetarians are now. When I was a child, vegetarianism was still highly unusual and regarded as cranky. Now, every restaurant and café has a vegetarian dish, and people are prepared to accept the fact that it is possible, even preferable, to live without meat on a daily basis. I hope that by the time my children are adults, raw foods will be equally integrated into our culture, and people will see the logic of eating food that has not been killed by the cooking process, just as they can now see the logic of not eating an animal which has been killed.

WHY EAT RAW FOODS?

Raw foods have a long and venerable history, dating right back to Biblical times. In *The Essene Gospel of Peace*, a reputedly overlooked book of the Bible, Jesus advocates eating raw foods.

> But I do say to you kill neither men nor beasts, nor yet the food which goes into your mouth. For if you eat living food, the same will quicken you, but if you kill your food, the dead food will kill you also. For life comes only from life, and from death comes always death. For everything which kills your foods, kills your bodies also. And everything which kills your bodies kills your souls also. And your bodies become what your foods are,

> even as your spirits, likewise, become what your thoughts are. Therefore eat not anything which fire, or frost, or water has destroyed, Fire burned, frozen and rotten foods will burn, freeze and rot your body also.

There have been many different raw food movements across the world during the twentieth century. However, in the early nineties, a whole new generation of raw foodists came on the scene, in particular in the USA, Australia, and the UK. Leading the way are David Wolfe and Nature's First Law, who operate out of sunny California and have the world's largest raw food shop and online superstore. David travels the world promoting raw foods and is a dynamic and inspiring speaker. There are countless others too who are just as passionate and work just as hard promoting the raw message, most notably Brian Clements who runs the Hippocrates Health Institute in Florida, and Gabriel Cousens who runs the Tree of Life in Arizona.

In 1930, the Swiss physician Dr. Paul Kautchakoff showed that eating cooked food causes leucocytosis, that is, an increase in white blood cells. Effectively, the body recognizes cooked food as a poison, and reacts accordingly, as it would with any poison entering the system. Cooked food is treated as a foreign body, so an immune response occurs; this does not happen when raw foods are eaten. Thus eating cooked foods regularly puts a huge strain on the immune system that eating raw foods does not, explaining why raw foodists tend to have more energy and be less susceptible to illness. Furthermore, the body cannot just distinguish raw food from cooked, but it recognizes how denatured the food is, and produces more leucocytes accordingly. For example, the body reacts more strongly to white flour than to whole-wheat flour, and junk foods such as hot dogs cause a reaction akin to food poisoning. Cooked foods can be eaten without causing leucocytosis if they are eaten with raw foods, and raw foods make up more than half of the meal. Another experiment in 1946 by Dr. Frances Pottenger, conducted on 900 cats, showed the degenerative effects of cooked foods. Half of the cats were fed raw meat and unpasteurized milk, the other half cooked meat and pasteurized milk. Over a ten-year period, the cats fed on raw foods thrived, while those on the cooked diet became progressively dysfunctional. Each generation of "cooked-food kittens" had poorer health and died younger.

From an ecological perspective, raw food is an incredible relief to the planet's resources, and a potential solution to world hunger. Raw food requires little or no packaging, and no processing, saving energy and emissions. No cooking also conserves energy, and saves money on fuels. Finally, all the waste is compostable and biodegradable, so not adding to the burden of rubbish that must be disposed of. Then there is the convenience aspect—although some of the recipes need time to prepare, it is possible to knock up a gourmet raw dinner in just a few minutes, and as for fruit, it is surely the ultimate convenience food. Furthermore, our healthcare system would save unimaginable amounts of money in not having to treat so many illnesses: raw foods have been used successfully to treat diseases such as cancer, heart disease, diabetes, skin and gut disorders. The Hippocrates Health Institute was founded in Boston, Massachussets in 1970 by Dr. Ann Wigmore, and has a long record of successfully treating people with life-threatening illnesses.

When we cook our foods, we lose a lot of the nutrients. Vitamin C and all the B group vitamins are heat-sensitive, and are considerably diminished by cooking. Enzymes are a much neglected part of nutrition, but just as vital to health as vitamins and minerals. We need them for every function in the body, yet they are completely destroyed by heat. We are born with a large store of enzymes, which gradually gets used up by life's processes. If we do not replace them with the enzymes found in live foods, our reserves get depleted, we age more quickly, and it gets harder for the body to maintain good health.

SO WHAT DO YOU EAT?

There is currently very little agreement within raw food circles as to what constitutes the correct diet. Most agree that fruitarianism (eating only plants with a seed) is inadvisable on a long-term basis. Some advocate making fruit the main part of your diet, others say to limit fruit and eat more green foods, vegetables and sprouts. Some say avoid juices, as they are not a natural part of the diet, others praise their healing and health-giving properties. Personally, I favor David Wolfe's Sunfood Triangle, which suggests a balance of fruit, green leafy vegetables, and fats such as nuts, seeds, olives, and avocado. I also believe that unfortunately, however well we eat, we cannot get all we need from our food. We lead fast-paced, pressured lives that take their toll on the body. We have to contend with huge amounts of environmental pollution inside and outside the home, that our grandparents did not have to cope with. More importantly, due to intensive agriculture policies, the soil is depleted and even organic produce does not contain the same levels of vitamins and minerals that it used to. To ensure the favorable health of my family, we add to our diet Klamath Lake blue-green algae, bee pollen, and Aloe Vera gel on a daily basis. None of these are supplements—all are foods in their own right—superfoods, in fact. They contain every nutrient and mineral that the body needs – theoretically you could live on them alone. As well as doing a great deal to ensure long term health and increased immunity, they boost energy levels considerably.

I am also an avid believer in drinking large quantities of water. Some raw foodists say that water is unnecessary with the diet, but I have always seen it as a food in its own right. On rising in the morning I drink over a quart of water, and continue to drink water and herb teas throughout the day. We commonly misinterpret thirst as hunger, and eat when in fact we are simply in need of liquid nourishment. Try gradually increasing the amount of liquid in your diet, and you will quite literally feel your body becoming more fluid. However, it is best not to drink with meals, as liquids weaken the digestive juices; drink before meals, or at least two hours afterwards. Contrary to popular belief, mineral water is not the best thing to drink. The minerals in bottled water are inorganic, and can also contain unwanted pollutants. Inorganic minerals are not bioavailable, and so form deposits in the body, leading to diseases such as hardening of the arteries. It is preferable to drink water purified by a reverse osmosis system, which is pure H_2O and nothing else.

Most health-conscious people are aware of the principles of food combining. Basically stated, this involves not mixing different classes of foods, such as proteins and starches, to aid digestion and absorption. These rules still apply when eating raw foods, but on a high raw diet you can be more relaxed about them, as the high enzyme content of the foods helps considerably with digestion. But don't go overboard, for instance by trying to create a traditional three-course dinner, and including lots of nuts, sprouted grains, vegetables, and fruits all in the same meal. Many people who are new to the diet experience problems with abdominal discomfort, bloating, and flatulence because their digestive systems, which have been weakened by decades of eating cooked foods, cannot cope with the powerful action of raw foods. This is one reason why it is best to introduce raw foods gradually, and to consider a course of colonics to help restore digestive action (see page 8).

Whatever your chosen diet, there are some foods you need to be very careful with. The arguments against meat and dairy products are too lengthy and involved for me to go into fully here. The treatment of animals in farming is increasingly being recognized as inhumane, and the industry itself is uneconomical and environmentally inefficient compared to the production of non-animal food sources. The consumption of meat and dairy products is a major factor in the cause of heart disease and cancer, the main killers in the Western world. And I have great difficulty with vegetarians who condemn meat eating, but happily consume dairy products that still involve great suffering for the animals concerned. If you feel you must eat animal products, buy only from organic sources, where the animals have had a better standard of care. For more information on the benefits of cutting out meat and dairy products from the diet, contact The Vegetarian Resource Group (see Resources on page 163).

One of the hardest foods to give up is bread. Wheat contains a natural opiate, and many people are addicted to bread because of its sedative effect. Unfortunately, wheat has been intensively farmed for too long now, and many people are finding they can no longer tolerate it. If I think back to my childhood, we often ate wheat at every meal: cereal for breakfast, sandwiches for lunch, pasta or pie for dinner, as well as wheat-based snacks in the form of chips, cakes, and cookies; it is no wonder my body has had enough and rejects it if I try to eat it now. People think of wholewheat organic bread as a healthy food, but consider how the wheat grain got to the plate: it was harvested, milled, made into bread, cooked, packaged, and then sent to the shops—how much lifeforce can be left in it by then? Far better to buy wheat grain and sprout it—most people who cannot tolerate wheat can eat it sprouted because of the enzymes released in the sprouting process, which turn the starches into more easily digestible sugars.

Although nuts form an essential part of a raw food diet, they should be eaten in small quantities only, and carefully prepared. When nuts are cooked, the fats in them become indigestible. Most commercial nut butters are made from heated nuts, although it is now possible to pick up gorgeous raw nut butters from many health food stores and natural food supermarkets. Nuts that we buy in most supermarkets are very often heat-treated to preserve them, even when bought in their shells. Cashews and brazils are never raw; the only way to be sure about other nuts is to check with the supplier. Peanuts are the worst nuts of all and should be avoided completely—they are highly indigestible and potentially carcinogenic (according to an FDA report), even organic ones—likewise pistachios, which contain a toxic fungus under their shells. All shelled nuts should be soaked before you use them, for two to twelve hours, to release the enzyme inhibitors

and make them more digestible. Sometimes it is acceptable to grind them to a fine powder before use, so they are already broken down and more easily utilized by the body. Seeds are easier on the system than nuts. Dried fruits are usually heat-treated, and for that reason shouldn't be eaten in large quantities. Olives are another food that sometimes aren't raw—try to buy fresh from a deli rather than in a jar or tinned.

It is best to avoid large quantities of soy, which contains an estrogen-mimicking chemical, and stresses the pancreas. Potatoes also cause great stress to the body, as they are so high in sugar. Rice cakes are thought of as healthy, but there is evidence that the puffed grains may be toxic. If you have an overwhelming craving for a food that you know isn't going to do you any favors, don't ignore it. The best way to overcome it is to prepare yourself a large green salad, and eat that first, or as an accompaniment. By filling up on the salad, you will be less likely to overeat on your treat, will minimize its toxic effects on your body, and maybe even reduce the craving for it.

In summer, raw food eating comes naturally and instinctively, but winter may seem more of a challenge. This is when cravings for cooked comfort foods are more likely to hit us hard. In reality, once you adjust to this way of eating, winter is no more difficult than any other time of year. In fact, you are less likely to feel the cold: when you eat hot food, your body has to work harder at regulating its internal temperature whereas when all your food is eaten at room temperature, it is easier for your body to retain its warmth. Some raw foodists find they revert to that child-like state of not feeling the cold at all. If you can't get over the urge for hot food, there are ways around it: gently heated soups, vegan burgers warmed in the dehydrator, and the extensive use of spices such as chili and ginger. I find myself eating more concentrated foods such as dehydrated goodies, nuts, and dried fruits. In summer, I gravitate towards seasonal fresh fruits that arrive in abundance.

Often raw food literature will make claims that children instinctively love raw foods over cooked foods. In my experience this is not true! All three of my children were raised on raw foods, but they will always prefer a rice cake to a dehydrated cracker, soy dessert to fruit pudding, or chips to salad. But this does not mean that we cannot educate their palates. I am constantly bartering with my four year old—"if you eat a banana you can have some soy dessert," or "eat some more cucumber and I'll give you another burger." All my children eat largely raw foods, and that is what they ask for because that is mostly what we have around the house. But on social occasions I never make a big deal out of it, and let them eat whatever vegan food is offered, so they do not feel too restricted. I always carry bananas, apples, and nuts with me for snacks, and if we are going somewhere where I know there will be foods they don't eat, I will bring their own treats with me. I also try to hide raw foods in cooked dishes, for example adding some raw vegetables, ground nuts, or sprouts to a dish at the end of cooking. If you are trying to add raw food to your children's diets, I cannot overemphasize the importance of striking a balance.

Many children in Western countries overeat on junk foods and suffer from malnourishment and constant illnesses. If you can encourage your children to eat just a little raw food a day, you are setting them up with beneficial habits for life. But don't worry if they are reluctant—don't starve them in an attempt to push the diet on to them! And consider the benefits of a supplement such as

blue-green algae that you can add to their drinks or favorite snacks, which will act as a safety net and ensure they are getting a dose of all the nutrients they need.

Finally, remember that raw foods alone cannot make us healthy. Exercise is essential and should form an integral part of your life. Yoga, walking, cycling, swimming, and rebounding are all excellent forms of exercise which are easy to incorporate into your daily routine. Rebounding is similar to trampolining and can be performed while you watch TV. At the same time, make sure that you include adequate rest and relaxation. Too many of us nowadays are constantly on the go, don't get enough sleep, and so don't allow the body time to recover and restore energy naturally. No matter how well we eat, if we don't give the body time for renewal, we become depleted and run down. Furthermore, research repeatedly shows that our mental state has a more profound effect on our health than our diet. Keep a positive outlook, a balanced, non-judgmental attitude to life, and seek to develop the self in all things.

Colonic hydrotherapy is a useful treatment, especially when you are embarking on a raw food diet. If your stomach is at all rotund, if you experience a lot of gas, if you are tired immediately after eating, you are likely to have impacted matter in the colon, which is often years old, and rots and decays, preventing efficient food absorption. You can have the best diet in the world, but if you aren't absorbing the food efficiently, it will do you no good. Have a course of colonics initially to clear you out, and then continue with them at regular intervals.

If you do fall ill, homeopathy is an excellent form of treatment. Find a reputable homeopath who can get to know you and your family, and will know the right remedies to prescribe when you need them. Homeopaths favor constitutional treatment, which builds up and strengthens the whole person, but can also prescribe acute treatments when necessary.

I consider the fundamental precepts of well-being to be a diet high in raw foods, superfoods, water, exercise, and rest, along with a positive outlook, regular colonics, and a sound relationship with a homeopath. I believe that if everyone made these simple lifestyle changes, levels of disease would drop dramatically as we all obtained superior levels of health. Furthermore, these measures are all inexpensive to implement, and our economy would benefit from a fitter workforce, and there would be huge savings for each of us in the cost of doctors' visits and prescription drugs.

I sincerely hope that you enjoy this book. It has come out of many years of my experience of eating raw, and finding foods that my family, friends, and I enjoy, as well as being easy and simple to prepare in our ever-busy lives. Most people I speak to who are interested in their health know that eating raw is beneficial, but don't know where to begin in adding raw foods to their diet. With little or no experience of gourmet raw cuisine, it is hard to move beyond the idea of raw foods being just salads and fruit. My wish is that this book achieves that purpose, and in doing so brings you closer to your true potential as a living being.

BASICS

Getting into raw foods needn't be complicated or confusing. It's a bit like learning a new language: once you've got the vocabulary and the grammar, it all starts to flow. In this preliminary chapter, we introduce you to all the exciting new equipment you can find in a raw kitchen, as well as a simple sprouting guide and shopping tips. As far as the equipment goes, none of it is essential: I was raw for many years before owning any more than a standard food processor and blender. But if you can afford to invest in these gadgets, it will make your raw cuisine more interesting and enjoyable.

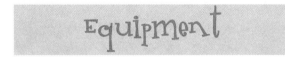

Equipment

A JUICER

Juicers are easy to find now, and you can buy one for as little as thirty dollars. However, I wouldn't recommend the cheaper models as they aren't very efficient, and you need a lot of fruit to make a decent amount of juice. At the other end of the scale the most popular models are The Champion Juicer, and The Green Power (see Resources, page 165). They are available in many health food stores and kitchenware shops and can cost upwards of three hundred dollars. However, they are built to last and are very efficient, and also can be used as homogenizers for making raw nut butters and more.

A DEHYDRATOR

If you are serious about eating more raw foods, I recommend a dehydrator as an essential purchase. A dehydrator is a simple box with a fan, a heating element, and trays for the food inside. It warms food at a very low temperature: it effectively cooks it without killing it, so technically it is still raw. Because it uses minimal heat, it takes a very long time to dry things out—anywhere up to twenty-four hours. I have a nine-tray dehydrator, which I use two or three times a week, and would not be able to feed my family without it. If you're finding it difficult to give up bread and treats, this is the way forward—for raw cookies and crackers, they are incomparable. They're equally indispensable for using up leftover produce—just slice it up, dry it out, and you've got some great snacks. I dry leafy greens, and then give them a quick whirl in the food processor to make a nutritious green powder to add to any dinner. If you do not have a dehydrator, you can use a conventional oven and have it on the lowest heat possible, with the door slightly open—this should heat the food at around the same temperature. You could leave dishes that need dehydrating for shorter periods, such as burgers, in a warm place, for instance an airing cupboard (although this probably would not work for cookies and breads, which need more drying). Dehydrated goods keep indefinitely if stored in an airtight container, in the refrigerator if possible.

RECOMMENDED FRUITS pineapple, pear, banana

RECOMMENDED VEGETABLES tomatoes, peppers, onions, greens

Or you can blend leftovers together, spread the mix on the trays, and make fruit and vegetable strips and chips. I make fruit strips out of bananas and whatever other fruits I've got lying around at the end of the week.

FOOD PROCESSOR

For serious mixing, the Vita-Mix is the connoisseur's machine. It performs virtually every food preparation task you can imagine with great speed and efficiency. Not only that, but the way the food is processed in a Vita-Mix increases bio-availability, so the body is able to absorb more nutrients. Like juicers and dehydrators, the Vita-Mix doesn't come cheap, but if good health is a real priority for you, or if you spend a lot of time on food preparation, it is definitely worth the investment. They are available from Vita-Mix (see Resources, page 165).

If a Vita-Mix is out of your price range, ideally you need a food processor with a mixer, a blender, and a grinder attachment. You will need quite a powerful blender—a lot of the cheaper models don't really do the job.

You also need a good sharp knife, a pair of small scissors for chopping herbs and dried fruits, a tablespoon and scales for measuring, a beater for making salad dressings, and a cook's thermometer for testing the temperature when gently heating dishes. I also find a set of standard measuring cups useful, especially when I am making sweet things (see page 139). You can find these in kitchen shops.

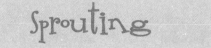

Sprouting

You can buy sprouters that are very efficient at raising sprouts, but I just use large jars that I keep next to the sink. Larger sprouts can just be rinsed once a day in the morning, but the smaller ones need to be done twice a day, especially in hot weather. There are many others to experiment with, but below is a list of the ones that I use the most. I always have some alfalfa on the go, and at least a couple of others. In hot weather, things sprout quicker. All nuts should be soaked for at least a few hours prior to use. This activates an enzyme, which makes them more easily digestible.

Put whatever it is you are sprouting in a large (one quart) jar, add approximately double the volume of water, and leave to soak for the stated time, preferably overnight. When you have finished soaking, rinse, and drain and leave to sprout, rinsing once or twice a day. Once your sprouts are ready, keep them in the refrigerator and eat them within a few days. Quantities given make approximately one jarful.

ALFALFA. One tablespoon, soak eight hours, sprout five to seven days. Alfalfa is an easy sprout to raise, and a staple of the raw food kitchen.

BUCKWHEAT. Five ounces, soak six hours, sprout two to three days. Buckwheat needs careful rinsing during soaking to stop it from turning slimy. Rinse every thirty to sixty minutes during soaking, and then rinse morning and night until ready.

CHICK PEA. Two to three ounces, soak ten to twelve hours, sprout three to four days.

LENTIL. Three ounces, soak ten to twelve hours, sprout three to four days.

MUNG BEAN. One and a half ounces, soak ten to twelve hours, sprout three to four days.

OAT GROATS. Four ounces, soak ten to twelve hours. Does not sprout—use within a day or two.

QUINOA. Five ounces, soak four hours, sprout two to three days. Quinoa needs careful rinsing before sprouting. Don't over soak, and rinse twice a day.

SUNFLOWER SEEDS. Four ounces, soak eight to ten hours, sprout two to three days. Another staple that is straightforward to sprout.

WHEAT GRAIN. One and a half ounces, soak ten to twelve hours, sprout three to four days. Wheat grain must be eaten within a day or two, or it starts to grow green, indigestible shoots.

Shopping

If you care about your food at all, you will already be eating organic. Organic food is the best option for so many reasons, not the least of which is that it is the only real alternative if we want to preserve our wonderful countryside, help restore the soil quality, and encourage wildlife. The vitamin, mineral, and enzyme count in organic produce is often as much as 50-percent higher than in non-organic produce, and by consuming organic foods, we avoid exposing ourselves to poisonous chemicals and potential carcinogens.

Since I began eating raw foods, the taste difference between organic and non-organic has become glaringly obvious; in my opinion, the flavors of organic food are far superior. At first sight organic food may seem more expensive, but it is worth paying the extra to get the better quality and nutritive value. Furthermore, what many people do not realize are the hidden costs of non-organic-farming that we pay for with our taxes: the subsidies that only non-organic farmers get, and the huge costs of cleaning up the damage done to the environment by agro-chemicals.

Most supermarkets are now well-stocked organically. But if possible, I believe it is better to avoid supermarkets, and support your local, independent shops. As people are becoming increasingly aware, the bigger corporations are less easy to hold accountable and more likely to manipulate the market. Ask your greengrocer if he can stock the most popular organic lines; most are happy to help, and can often undercut the supermarkets by a great deal. Wholefood stores are always ready to advise on items, are generally more knowledgeable than supermarket staff, and often have better-quality produce. Wherever you shop, try to buy locally grown, seasonal produce whenever possible—not only does it contribute to the economy of this country, but it will be much tastier and fresher than something which has travelled miles to get here, causing unnecessary pollution on the way.

If you are serious about adopting this way of eating, you would do well to start purchasing ingredients in bulk. Items such as nuts and dried fruits can be expensive, but if you buy one pound at a time, the price is reduced drastically. These items keep well, so there is no need to worry about over-stocking, and as well as saving money, you cut down on packaging. Your health food shop should be willing to order items in for you.

What to Buy

Following is a brief guide to building a raw store cupboard. Your main staples are going to be fresh fruit and vegetables, but there are a few other specialty ingredients you may want to have fun getting to know. They shouldn't be hard to track down, but can make all the difference in turning your cuisine from a standard affair to something altogether classier.

FRUIT

Buy locally grown produce, in season whenever possible.

Staples: apples, bananas, oranges, pears, grapes, lemons, dates (try and buy fresh dates as opposed to dried wherever possible).

Plus there are a whole host of exotic fruits to discover, including mango, papaya, guava, lychee, plantain, kumquats, star fruit, prickly pear, and passion fruit.

VEGETABLES

Again, for superior quality, buy locally grown, in-season produce. However, many vegetables can be difficult to digest raw.

Staples: broccoli, cabbage, carrots, onions, avocados, spinach, lettuce, celery, cucumber, tomatoes, peppers (not green ones, they are unripe and hard on the digestion), mushrooms, beet, zucchini, radishes, corn, green beans, olives.

There is a wide variety of leafy greens which should start to form an important part of your diet, such as arugula, spinach, endives, kale, bok choy, arugala, watercress, and chicory. Or try some of the more unusual vegetables such as daikon radish, Jerusalem artichoke, celeriac, fennel, or kohlrabi.

SEA VEGETABLES

An essential part of anyone's diet. They contain more minerals than any other kind of food, as well as many vital vitamins. For example, dulse contains fifteen times more calcium than cow's milk.

Dulse, arame, nori (flakes and sheets), kelp, wakame, hijiki.

HERBS AND SPICES

Essential for turning a plain dish into something special.

Fresh – ginger, garlic, red chili, parsley, and as many other fresh herbs as you can afford, or preferably, grow.

Dried – cinnamon, cumin, garam masala, Chinese five spice, paprika, nutmeg, and cloves.

NUTS

Walnuts, almonds, cashews, coconut (fresh), brazils, hazelnuts, pecans, pine nuts.

SEEDS

Sesame, sunflower, pumpkin, hemp, flax, alfalfa (for sprouting only), raw tahini.

DRIED FRUIT

Avoid fruits that have been sulphured. Instead, use organically grown, sun-dried fruits such as light apricots, pears, raisins, dates, apricots, figs, and prunes.

GRAINS

Wheat, oat groats, quinoa, buckwheat.

BEANS AND PULSES

Lentil, chick pea, mung bean.

OILS

Flax oils are raw, but cold pressed oils aren't, necessarily.

Flax (or hemp), extra virgin olive oil.

SWEETENERS

Molasses, apple concentrate, unpasteurized honey, agave nectar, yacon syrup.

Molasses is not raw, but is packed full of minerals, which is why I like to use it occasionally. Apple concentrate isn't raw either, but it isn't too highly processed, comes from a natural fruit source, contains no additives, and is relatively inexpensive. It is also the least worst option for your teeth, not being as sticky as syrups. Unpasteurized honey is raw, but I prefer not to use it as it is an animal by-product. Young children should avoid unpasteurized raw honey due to potential infant botulism.

PICKLES

Look out for pickles that are unpasteurized. These food items should be raw and naturally fermented. These include:

Sauerkraut, gherkins, pickled onions.

FLAVORINGS

APPLE CIDER VINEGAR – There is a raw one made by Braggs, but whatever you buy, make sure it is unpasteurized.

BRAGGS LIQUID AMINOS – Braggs Liquid Aminos has a similar flavor to soy sauce, and is made from hydrolyzed vegetable protein. It is best to use in moderation, as it allegedly contains naturally occurring monosodium glutamate.

CAROB POWDER – Carob powder is made from grinding the pods of the carob tree. Most carob powders in the wholefood stores have been roasted or toasted, but it is possible to buy raw carob from a specialist raw supplier. Or look out for whole carob pods which make a tasty healthy snack.

CHINESE 5-SPICE POWDER – A zesty combination of Asian flavorings incorporating equal parts of cinnamon, fennel, star anise, cloves, and Szechwan pepper. This product can be found in most supermarkets.

LIVE SOY YOGURT – Contains beneficial probiotics.

MISO – Get unpasteurized. Although not strictly a raw food, because of the enzymatic activity, it is a living food.

NUTRITIONAL YEAST FLAKES – Adds a cheesy taste to foods, high in B vitamins and minerals, not raw.

SUN-DRIED TOMATOES – These may not actually be sun dried! I buy them in packets, then marinate them myself. For recipes, I use dehydrated tomatoes.

TAMARI OR SHOYU – Tamari has a more intense flavor, shoyu is slightly mellower. Whenever I have specified tamari in a recipe, shoyu can be substituted if you prefer.

VANILLA EXTRACT – Not vanilla essence, which is a cheap imitation.

Nutrients

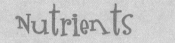

I am not a qualified nutritionist, and this is by no means an exhaustive list, but a summary of where the most important nutrients for health can be found in a raw food diet.

FATS

Many people avoid fats for fear of putting on weight. But it is the type of fats that they consume that makes them unhealthy—uncooked fats are metabolized by the body in a different way, and are essential for good health. Fats are a vital part of the diet, particularly the essential fatty acids.

Nuts and seeds, avocados, olives and oils. The best sources of essential fatty acids are flaxseed and hemp seed.

PROTEIN

Mother's milk contains only 2-percent protein, and babies do a massive amount of growing fed on this alone. This would indicate that we don't need as much protein in the diet as we are led to believe.

Sources: all nuts and seeds, especially pine nuts, walnuts, pumpkin seeds, and sunflower seeds. Sprouts, especially buckwheat, quinoa, and wheat. Soy and miso.

Minerals

CALCIUM

In one tablespoon of sesame seeds, there is more than eight times the amount of calcium than there is in a cup of cow's milk! Weight for weight, green leafy vegetables contain roughly double the amount of calcium as cow's milk.

All nuts and seeds, especially sesame, flax, hazelnuts, almonds, brazils. Chick peas, tofu, garlic, figs, and leafy greens. All sea vegetables, especially dulse and kelp.

CHROMIUM

Wheat, apples, broccoli, corn, mushrooms, onion, pears.

COPPER

Nuts and seeds, especially pecans and walnuts. Buckwheat.

IRON

One ounce of flaxseed contains more than double the RDA of iron.

Quinoa, tofu. Nuts and seeds, especially flaxseed, pumpkin seeds, sesame seeds, pine nuts. All leafy greens especially parsley. Sea vegetables.

MAGNESIUM

All nuts and seeds, especially pumpkin seeds. Buckwheat, rye. Sea vegetables.

PHOSPHOROUS

All nuts and seeds, especially pumpkin seeds. Buckwheat, quinoa, rye, wheat, soy. Sea vegetables.

POTASSIUM

Grains, especially buckwheat, quinoa, rye, and wheat. Chick peas, lentils, mung beans, soy. All nuts and seeds, especially pistachios. Avocados, bananas, dates, raisins. Parsley, spinach. Sea vegetables.

SELENIUM

Brazil nuts.

ZINC

Buckwheat, quinoa, miso, all nuts and seeds

especially pumpkin seeds and sesame seeds. Leafy greens.

Vitamins

VITAMIN A

Apricots, melons, papaya, sharon fruit, beet, broccoli, carrots, leafy greens, sweet potato. Nori.

B VITAMINS

Leafy greens, nutritional yeast flakes, sea vegetables.

B_{12}

There is much controversy over how a healthy vegan gets their B_{12}. The only vegan sources of this vitamin are sea vegetables, Aloe vera and blue-green algae, but many people believe that a healthy body will manufacture enough to meet its requirements.

VITAMIN C

All fruits and vegetables, especially guavas, kiwi, papaya, strawberries, blackcurrants, broccoli, cauliflower, peppers, kale.

VITAMIN E

Almonds, brazil nuts, hazelnuts, cucumber.

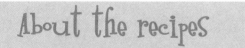

About the recipes

Each and every recipe here are dishes that I regularly serve my family. Although many require advance preparation, none are so labor intensive as to be unrealistic to incorporate into your daily menu. All quantities given work for me, but with raw foods there are no hard and fast rules; you can vary ingredients, for instance substituting one vegetable for another, or one nut for another. Or if you are particularly fond of an ingredient, you can add extra (more garlic, extra almonds). Some raw food tastes are "acquired;" as your taste buds become attuned to this way of eating, you can experiment with some of the more unusual dishes. Keep an open mind, and don't expect it to taste the same as cooked food—raw pizza, for example, is a real treat for us, but only a distant cousin to the Italian version. Raw foods are packed with goodness, no empty calories, and so are often more intense in their flavor; you may well find you need to eat much smaller portions to satisfy yourself. Wherever possible, quantities given serve one only. This should make it easy for you to try out dishes on your own, or to multiply the ingredients to cater for whatever numbers necessary. All leftovers should be stored in the refrigerator, with the exception of dehydrated goodies, which must be kept in an airtight container.

Conclusion

There's never been such an exciting time to get into raw foods. There are so many resources around now, and so much support available from established raw experts. There are so many amazing new raw foods appearing on the market to give your meals that little something extra. So please, take advantage of what this book has to offer: try out some recipes, and create your own variations according to what's in season or what you are craving today. Allow more raw foods into your diet, and open a doorway to living a life of abundant health and happiness.

1. Breakfast

Raw Muesli

Sweet Buckwheat Cereal

Savory Buckwheat Cereal

Sweet Oatmeal

Savory Oatmeal

RaW Muesli

Yield: Serves two

Raw fooders tend not to eat breakfast, so we are more likely to serve these dishes as a lunch or snack. I usually just have juice in the morning; if you want some solid food, plain fruit is a sensible idea.

You may find it easier to cut dates and apricots into small pieces with scissors, rather than using a knife. If you don't have fresh coconut, desiccated is an acceptable alternative.

1 ½ oz	wheat sprouts (page 13)
2 tbsp	sunflower sprouts (page 13)
2 tbsp	raisins
1 tbsp	hemp seeds
1 tbsp	grated fresh coconut
1 tbsp	sesame seeds
1 tbsp	dried apricots, chopped
1 tbsp	dates, chopped

Stir all the ingredients together until they are thoroughly mixed, and serve with almond milk (page 156).

PER SERVING

Calories	488
Fat	19.3 g
Carbohydrate	69.6 g
Fiber	9.1 g

Contains at least 25% of the RDA for: Iron, Vitamins B1, B6 and Folate

Sweet Buckwheat Cereal

If you have a cook's thermometer, you can warm cereals, making sure the temperature stays below 117°F. You will need to add extra water gradually, while stirring continuously.

8 oz	sprouted buckwheat (page 13)
1 tbsp	tahini
1 tsp	cinnamon
1 tbsp	apple concentrate
2 tbsp	raisins
2 tbsp	boiling water
1 tbsp	sunflower seeds
1 tbsp	pumpkin seeds

In the food processor, break down the buckwheat until the grains are a creamy mash. Add the tahini, cinnamon, and apple concentrate, and process again to make a thick batter. While the machine is running, pour in the water, and process for another minute. Turn the machine off, and stir in the raisins, pumpkin seeds, and sunflower seeds with a spoon. Serve immediately, while warm.

Yield: Serves two

Someone who doesn't have so many toxins in their system wakes in the morning with plenty of energy, and no immediate desire for food. The digestive system doesn't really get going until midday, so the later in the morning you can leave it before eating, the easier it is on your body.

PER SERVING

Calories	447
Fat	13.2 g
Carbohydrate	71.9 g
Fiber	3.1 g

Contains at least 25% of the RDA for: Iron, Vitamins B1, B3, B6, Folate and Vitamin E

Savory Buckwheat Cereal

Yield: Serves two

Buckwheat is actually a herb; the part that we sprout is the seed.

I discovered this when making buckwheat cookies—the mixture was just as appetizing as the finished version!

8 oz	sprouted buckwheat (page 13)
1 tbsp	extra virgin olive oil
1 tsp	miso
2 tbsp	fresh parsley, chopped finely
$^1/_4$	onion, chopped finely
2 tbsp	boiling water
1 tbsp	pumpkin seeds
1 tbsp	sunflower seeds

PER SERVING

Calories	412
Fat	14.7 g
Protein	14.2 g
Carbohydrate	59.1 g
Fiber	3.0 g

Contains at least 25% of the RDA for: Iron, Vitamins B1, B3, B6, Folate, Vitamins C and E

In the food processor, break down the buckwheat until it forms a creamy mash. Add the extra virgin olive oil, miso, parsley, and onion, and process again to make a thick batter. Next, pour in the water and blend until you have a creamy purée. Turn the machine off, and stir in the pumpkin and sunflower seeds with a spoon. Serve immediately.

sweet oatmeal

Rolled oats, usually used in oatmeal, are heated during the processing, and have had some of the goodness removed. Oat groats are simply the hulled grain, and are available from wholefood stores. They are about the same size as rice grains, and must be soaked for eight to twelve hours, although they do not sprout.

4 oz	oat groats, soaked overnight
1 tbsp	apple concentrate
1 tbsp	flaxseed oil
1 tsp	cinnamon
4 fl oz	boiling water
2 tbsp	raisins
2 tbsp	chopped nuts

Put the oat groats in the food processor and process for a couple of minutes, until the individual grains are no longer discernible and they have formed a thick mash. Add the apple concentrate, flax oil, and cinnamon, and blend again. Then pour in the water, and process to a thick creamy purée. Turn the machine off, and stir in the raisins and nuts with a spoon. Serve immediately, while warm.

Yield: Serves two

Research repeatedly shows that a diet high in nutrients and low in calories reduces the risk of serious disease and slows the aging process.

PER SERVING

Calories	462
Fat	20.6 g
Protein	10.3 g
Carbohydrate	62.5 g
Fiber	5.5 g

Contains at least 25% of the RDA for: Iron, Vitamin B1, Folate and Vitamin E

Savory Oatmeal

Garlic, miso, and oats together give terrific protection against winter illnesses. Garlic was eaten by Roman gladiators to improve their strength in the stadium.

This makes a warming lunch on a cold winter's day. If you are a garlic fan, try crushing a few cloves into the mixture.

4 oz	oats, soaked overnight
1 tbsp	carrot, grated
1 tbsp	onion, chopped finely
1 tbsp	fresh parsley, chopped finely
1 tbsp	nutritional yeast
1 tsp	miso
1 tbsp	flax oil
4 fl oz	boiling water

Put the oats in the food processor, and process for a couple of minutes, until the individual grains are no longer discernible, but have formed a thick mash. Add all other ingredients except water, and process for another minute. Then pour in the water, and keep the machine turning until you have a creamy batter. Serve immediately.

PER SERVING

Calories	326
Fat	10.6 g
Protein	14.1 g
Carbohydrate	46.3 g
Fiber	8.2 g

Contains at least 25% of the RDA for: Iron, Vitamin B1 and Folate

2. Soups

Sunshine Soup

Tomato Soup

Mushroom Soup

Thai Soup

Creamy Carrot and Spinach Soup

Coconut Soup

Sunshine Soup

A basic recipe—you can vary it with your own favorite vegetables.

Yield: Serves two

3	tomatoes
1	yellow pepper
$^1/_2$	avocado
2 oz	spinach
8 fl oz	carrot juice
1 tbsp	flax oil
1 tsp	miso
$^1/_2$ inch	piece fresh ginger
1	clove garlic
$^1/_2$	red chili

Soups can be warmed gently, either by using boiling water where water is stated in the recipe, or by heating in a pan, using a cook's thermometer to check the temperature (no higher than 117°F). None of these soups suit being heated to boiling point.

Roughly chop the tomatoes, pepper, avocado, and spinach. Put everything in the blender, and purée until all ingredients have been broken down and you have a smooth, lump-free soup.

PER SERVING

Calories	424
Fat	27.3 g
Carbohydrate	36.0 g
Fiber	10.3 g

Contains at least 25% of the RDA for: Iron, Calcium, Vitamins B1, B2, B3, B6, Folate, Vitamins C, A and E

Tomato Soup

Yield: Serves two

Tomatoes contain lycopene, an antioxidant which helps protect against cancer. The darker the tomato, the higher its lycopene content.

Adding the avocado makes a creamier soup.

12	tomatoes
1	stick celery
2	clove garlic
4	dates
2 tbsp	fresh basil
2 tbsp	nutritional yeast flakes
2 tbsp	Braggs Liquid Aminos (page 15)
8 fl oz	water
1	avocado (optional)

Roughly chop tomatoes and celery (and avocado if you are using it). Put everything in the blender, and purée until smooth.

PER SERVING

Calories	220
Fat	2.2 g
Carbohydrate	37.7 g
Fiber	8.4 g

Contains at least 25% of the RDA for: Iron, Vitamins B1, B2, B3, B6, Folate, Vitamins C, A and E

Mushroom Soup

Shiitake mushrooms may be difficult to find but they do add a real depth of flavor to this soup.

Yield: Serves two

Shiitake mushrooms have immune system boosting properties, and have been used in the treatment of AIDS.

4 oz	shiitake mushrooms
12	chestnut mushrooms
1	red pepper
4 tbsp	fresh parsley
4 tbsp	almond butter (page 34)
2 tsp	miso
2 tbsp	flax oil
24 fl oz	water

Roughly chop the mushrooms and pepper. Put everything in the blender and blend to a smooth purée.

PER SERVING

Calories	382
Fat	33.3 g
Carbohydrate	10.0 g
Fiber	5.1 g

Contains at least 25% of the RDA for: Iron, Vitamins B2, B6, Folate and Vitamins C, A and E

Thai Soup

This is one to serve to impress your guests! If you can't get fresh coconut you can use eight fluid ounces of coconut milk instead, but coconut milk is not raw.

Yield: Serves two

I really missed eating Thai food for a while, until I realized that the secret was all in the delicate balance of the flavors, and that I would be able to recreate that in a raw dish, using the same ingredients. Thai soups are only lightly cooked anyway, so as not to destroy the tastes.

PER SERVING

Calories	409
Fat	24.0 g
Carbohydrate	39.9 g
Fiber	12.1 g

Contains at least 25% of the RDA for: Iron, Calcium, Vitamins B1, B3, B6, Folate and Vitamins C, A and E

6	mushrooms
6	tomatoes
2	clove garlic
1 inch	piece fresh ginger
1	lemon grass stick
2	red chili
4	dates
6	lime leaves
	juice 2 limes
	small bunch coriander
4 oz	fresh coconut, chopped
8 oz	spinach
1	apple
2 tbsp	tamari
	water to blend

Roughly chop the mushrooms and tomatoes. Put everything in the blender together, and purée thoroughly for a couple of minutes, making sure there are no bits of herb or spice left unprocessed. Serve garnished with sprouts such as mung bean or lentil.

Creamy Carrot and Spinach Soup

Yield: Serves two

Spinach is a first rate source of iron. Two out of three women are iron deficient.

Cooked carrot and spinach soup was a favorite of mine. The sweetness of the carrots complements the slightly bitter spinach perfectly.

6	large carrots, chopped
12 oz	spinach
1	onion
4	cloves garlic
1	apple, chopped
2	avocado, cubed
2 tsp	miso
2 tbsp	flaxseed oil
2 tsp	kelp
16 fl oz	water
3 oz	mung bean sprouts (page 13)

PER SERVING

Calories	638
Fat	41.9 g
Carbohydrate	52.3 g
Fiber	22.9 g

Contains at least 25% of the RDA for: Iron, Calcium, Vitamins B1, B2, B3, B6, Folate and Vitamins C, A and E

Put everything apart from the sprouts in the blender and purée until smooth. Mix the sprouts in by hand—sprinkle a few on the top as a garnish.

Coconut Soup

This is a very rich, warming soup. I practically lived on it for a good while about ten years ago. Like all raw soups, it is so quick and easy to prepare (just as quick as heating up the contents of a can!). The richness of the coconut contrasts beautifully with the sharpness of the celery and carrot.

Yield: Serves two small portions

You can make your own creamed coconut (page 144), or use shop bought, which is not raw.

6 oz	creamed coconut
1	red chili
2	clove garlic
1/2 inch	piece fresh ginger
1/2	onion
4	dates
16 fl oz	water
2 oz	lentil sprouts (page 13)
2	stick celery, sliced thinly
2	carrot, sliced thinly

Put everything apart from the sprouts, celery, and carrot into the blender. Blend for a couple of minutes until you have a thick purée. Transfer to a bowl, and using a spoon, stir the sprouts, celery, and carrot into the coconut sauce.

PER SERVING

Calories	459
Fat	31.9 g
Carbohydrate	37.0 g
Fiber	4.8 g

Contains at least 25% of the RDA for: Iron, Folate, Vitamins C, A and E

3. Nut Butters, Dips, Dressings, and Sauces

Nut Butters

Carole's Carrot Dip

Reuben's Dip

Guacamole

Red Hot Pepper Dip

Tahini Dip

Raw Hummus

Sunflower Pâté

Broccoli and Rosemary Dip

Mushroom Pâté

Tomato Ketchup

Miso-Mayo Dressing

Ultimate Dressing

Umeboshi Dressing

Nikki's Dressing

Easy Avocado Mayo

Almond Mayo

Satay Sauce

Barbeque Sauce

Salsa

Pasta Sauce

Tahini and Miso Gravy

Grated "Cheese"

Melted "Cheese"

Nut Butters

Few, if any, of the nut butters sold in the shops are raw. You can break down nuts in a Champion, Vita-Mix, or any other heavy-duty juicer, and although they become more homogenized than ground nuts, they don't really qualify as nut butter. To put seeds through the Champion, you need to grind them first. However, if you have time and patience, you can make a very passable nut butter in your food processor. Again, if you are using seeds you must grind them first. I always have tahini and almond butter in my refrigerator for use in recipes. Brazils and macadamias work very well (probably because they are already heat-treated).

Put the nuts or seeds in the food processor and turn it on maximum speed for five to ten minutes, stopping regularly to stir it and make sure it is evenly mixed. As the nuts and seeds break down, the friction in the machine will cause them to heat up, which is obviously undesirable. Once it starts to get warm, turn it off and leave for half an hour to an hour, then return to it, and process for a further five to ten minutes. Repeat this process throughout the day. Gradually, it should turn from a powder to a paste, and finally a butter. The longer you persevere with it, the runnier the end result. Store in the refrigerator.

I had been on a high raw diet for years but one of my major stumbling blocks was nut butters. Then a friend told me about this method, which is time consuming, but also much more economical.

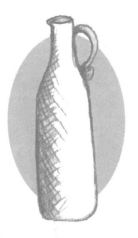

Carole's Carrot Dip

Yield: About one cup

Carole is a friend who inspired this dish when she told me that she makes dips simply by blending up whatever vegetables she has on hand with some tahini. This is the best combination I have found, and I often make it when I have a lot of people visiting, as it is cheap and easy to make in bulk.

This makes a thick, zesty dip or spread. It's so superb, you can just eat it as it is! I use it in Roll-Ups (page 86), or as a dip with raw vegetables.

1 ¹/₂	large carrots
¹/₂	large onion
1 tbsp	chopped fresh dill
1 tbsp	lemon juice
1 tbsp	tamari
1 tbsp	extra virgin olive oil
2 tbsp	tahini
1 tbsp	water

Roughly chop the carrot and onion. Put everything in the blender and blend for a couple of minutes until you have a smooth purée.

PER 15 g TABLESPOON	
Calories	19
Fat	1.5 g
Protein	0.4 g
Carbohydrate	0.9 g
Fiber	0.4 g

Reuben's Dip

Yield: About one cup

I make this for my son as it's packed full of nourishment. He has it spread on bread, or as a dip for cucumber and carrot sticks. Add water to reach the desired consistency—a little will give you a very thick spread. Add a little more if you're using it as a dip, and more again to make a nutritious, creamy salad dressing.

2 tbsp	tahini
1 tbsp	miso
2 tbsp	nutritional yeast flakes
2 tbsp	flax seeds, ground
2 tsp	vinegar
1 tsp	kelp
	water

Put everything in a small bowl (I usually use a teacup), and using a hand whisk, blend it all together.

Miso is a Japanese food, used in macrobiotic cookery. It's traditionally made from fermented soy beans and/or rice, is full of enzymes and B vitamins, and is effective at warding off illness. Try stirring a teaspoon into a cup of boiling water to make a warming savory drink.

PER 15 g TABLESPOON	
Calories	53
Fat	3.4 g
Protein	2.9 g
Carbohydrate	2.7 g
Fiber	1.9 g

Guacamole

Guacamole is one raw dish that everyone has heard of and is a staple for raw fooders. Most of us eat avocados every day as an essential source of fat in the diet. Guacamole is very versatile: spread it on crackers, use it as a dip for raw vegetables, or add it to roll-ups (page 86).

Yield: About one cup

If you're preparing guacamole in advance, store it with an avocado stone in it to prevent it turning an unappetizing brown color.

1	large avocado
1	large tomato
1 tbsp	onion
1 tbsp	fresh coriander
1 tbsp	fresh parsley
1	garlic clove
1 tsp	kelp
1/2	red chili
1 tbsp	tamari
	juice 1 lemon

PER 15 g TABLESPOON	
Calories	14
Fat	1.2 g
Protein	0.3 g
Carbohydrate	0.4 g
Fiber	0.4 g

Roughly chop the avocado and tomato. Blend everything except the tamari and lemon juice in the food processor. When you have no lumps left, add the tamari and lemon juice, and process for another minute, until the mixture starts to thicken.

Yield: About one cup

Cumin is a spice
commonly used in
curry powder, but I use
it frequently on its own
to add an exotic aroma
to a dish.

PER 15 g TABLESPOON	
Calories	76
Fat	6.7 g
Protein	2.1 g
Carbohydrate	2.1 g
Fiber	1.2 g

Yield: About one cup

Made from ground
sesame seeds, tahini is
very high in calcium,
and an essential part of
a raw vegan diet. It has
a neutral taste that
goes well with sweet
and savory dishes, and
can be used in place of
butter and margarine
as a spread.

PER 15 g TABLESPOON	
Calories	61
Fat	5.9 g
Protein	1.9 g
Carbohydrate	0.2 g
Fiber	0.8 g

Red Hot Pepper Dip

*This makes a vibrant, spicy dip or spread. Great for crackers,
crudites and Roll-Ups (page 86).*

3	red peppers
1	stick celery
5 oz	tahini
1 tsp	ground cumin
1 tbsp	tamari
2 tbsp	extra virgin olive oil
2	cloves garlic
1	red chili

Roughly chop the peppers and celery. Put everything in the
blender, and process for a couple of minutes until you have a
thick purée.

Tahini Dip

*This is simple but very palatable—suitable for when you're in a
hurry, or have to cater for large groups. If you're a garlic fan, add
some, crushed. It makes a wonderful spread for crackers or creamy
dip for crudites.*

8 oz	tahini
2 tbsp	lemon juice
1 tbsp	tamari
4 tbsp	water

Blend everything in the food processor, or manually with a
hand whisk.

Raw Hummus

If you love hummus, try this raw version, which uses the same ingredients, but made from sprouted chick peas rather than cooked ones. Raw chick peas are quite difficult to digest so eat this with a simple salad or vegetable dips—avoid mixing with crackers or chips unless you have very efficient digestion.

Yield: About one and a half cups

If you fancy a snack lunch, any of the dips in this section make a delicious light meal served with an array of crudites such as mushroom, broccoli, cucumber, carrot, or pepper. Good for packed lunches.

8 oz	sprouted chick peas (page 13)
2 tbsp	tahini
2 tbsp	extra virgin olive oil
1 tbsp	lemon juice
1 tbsp	tamari
2	cloves garlic
2 tbsp	water

Put everything in the blender, and blend for couple of minutes until you have a thick purée.

PER 15 g TABLESPOON	
Calories	36
Fat	2.9 g
Protein	1.0 g
Carbohydrate	1.6 g
Fiber	0.4 g

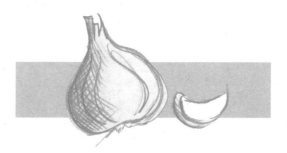

Sunflower Pâté

Yield: About two cups

This can be used as a dip, to make Roll-Ups (page 86), or stuffed in peppers.

You can use any combination of vegetables that you have on hand: broccoli, mushroom, celery, carrot. Or replace the sunflower seeds with four ounces of pumpkin seeds, soaked overnight.

10 oz	mixed vegetables
small bunch	parsley
$1/2$	onion
4 oz	sunflower seeds, sprouted (page 13)
2 tbsp	flaxseed oil
2 tbsp	lemon juice
1 tbsp	tamari
1 tsp	ground cumin
$1/2$	red chili
2	cloves garlic

PER 15 g TABLESPOON	
Calories	14
Fat	0.7 g
Protein	0.5 g
Carbohydrate	1.7 g
Fiber	0.2 g

Chop vegetables, parsley, and onion roughly. Put everything in the food processor, and process for a couple of minutes until you have a smooth purée.

Yield: About one cup

"There's rosemary, that's for remembrance" is a line from Shakespeare's Hamlet; scientists have shown that rosemary does actually act as a stimulant to the memory.

Broccoli and Rosemary Dip

The rosemary adds an unusual tang to this recipe, which goes well in Nori Roll-Ups (page 86).

I	large head broccoli
1/2	onion
I	avocado
2	sprigs rosemary
I tbsp	tamari
2 tbsp	extra virgin olive oil
2 tbsp	nutritional yeast flakes

Roughly chop the broccoli, onion, and avocado. Remove the rosemary leaves from the stem; discard the stem. Blend everything in the food processor for a couple of minutes. If you like a bit of texture, you can leave it a bit lumpy with the broccoli discernible; or you can process longer until it is a smooth purée.

PER 15 g TABLESPOON	
Calories	20
Fat	1.6 g
Protein	0.7 g
Carbohydrate	0.6 g
Fiber	0.5 g

DRIED TOMATOES

I find my dehydrator invaluable for making dried tomatoes, which add depth to any tomato dish. If you can't dry your own, you can buy them in packets, or simply use tomato purée instead. However, tomato purée is not raw, and when used in large amounts, such as in this recipe, I find it can have quite a processed taste. Replace one ounce dried tomatoes with two tablespoons tomato purée.

Yield: About one cup

You may find it handy to keep seeds ready ground, stored in jars in the refrigerator. I always have at least almonds, flaxseed, and sesame seeds on hand. In many recipes you can substitute ground seeds or nuts for nut butters; the result will be slightly different in texture but perfectly acceptable. Grinding your own is much cheaper than buying nut butters from the shops, which are not raw anyway.

PER 15 g TABLESPOON	
Calories	48
Fat	4.1 g
Protein	1.8 g
Carbohydrate	1.0 g
Fiber	0.6 g

Mushroom Pâté

This is fantastic on crackers such as Raw-Vita (page 57) or garlic crackers (page 54).

8	mushrooms
1	stick celery
bunch	parsley
2	cloves garlic
1/2	red chili
1 tbsp	miso
2 oz	sunflower seeds, ground
2 oz	pumpkin seeds, ground
3 oz	sesame seeds, ground
2 tbsp	water

Roughly chop the mushrooms, celery, and parsley. Put everything in the food processor apart from the water, and process until smooth. Pour in the water, and process for another minute.

Yield: About one cup

PER 15 g TABLESPOON	
Calories	9
Fat	0.0 g
Protein	0.3 g
Carbohydrate	1.9 g
Fiber	0.3 g

Yield: About one and a half cups

For variety, add some chopped herbs to this recipe: chives go particularly well.

There are some very palatable soy-based mayonnaises on the market if you don't have the time or inclination to make your own.

PER 15 g TABLESPOON	
Calories	55
Fat	4.8 g
Protein	1.4 g
Carbohydrate	1.6 g
Fiber	0.4 g

Tomato Ketchup

This is first class—you can use it as a dip or a salad dressing (page 72), not just as an accompaniment to burgers and sausages.

3	tomatoes
1/2	onion
2 oz	dried tomatoes
4	dates
1 tbsp	vinegar
1 tsp	tamari
1 tsp	kelp

Roughly chop the tomatoes and onion. Put everything in the blender, and purée until smooth.

Miso-Mayo Dressing

The amount of water you use in this recipe will also depend on the type of mayonnaise that you use. I include two raw recipes in the book, on page 47.

2 tbsp	miso
4 tbsp	almond mayonnaise (page 47)
2 tbsp	nutritional yeast flakes
	juice 1 lemon
	water to mix

In a small bowl, whisk together all ingredients with a hand whisk. Add water drop by drop to reach desired consistency. This makes a satisfying creamy salad dressing.

ultimate Dressing

Yield: About one cup

Dill is my favorite herb. It has a distinctive refreshing flavor that can transform an average dish into something more memorable. It is said to be very beneficial for the digestion, and a help to Irritable Bowel Syndrome (IBS) sufferers.

This has everything in it! It makes the creamiest, yummiest dressing ever. It makes quite a lot so you can store it in the refrigerator and use for a few salads, or as a creamy sauce over vegetables. Experiment with different herbs to see which you prefer.

bunch	parsley
2 tbsp	fresh tarragon, basil, dill—your choice
$\frac{1}{2}$	onion
2 oz	almond butter (page 34)
$\frac{1}{2}$	avocado
2 tbsp	extra virgin olive oil
I tsp	tamari
I tbsp	lemon juice
I tsp	vinegar
I tbsp	nutritional yeast flakes
I tsp	kelp
4 fl oz	water

Put everything in the blender and process for a few minutes until the mixture starts to thicken.

PER 15 g TABLESPOON	
Calories	17
Fat	1.5 g
Protein	0.5 g
Carbohydrate	0.4 g
Fiber	0.3 g

Umeboshi Dressing

Yield: About one and a half cups

Kelp seaweed is sold in powder or granular form, and has a salty, fishy taste. It has the highest mineral count of any food, and is particularly important as a source of iodine. Try and get some seaweed in your diet every day by adding just half a teaspoon of kelp to your dinner; no more or you can overdose on iodine.

Umeboshi paste is a very pungent, salty substance, made from Japanese pickled plums. It is good for the digestion and is used in macrobiotic cookery. This dressing will add a distinctive tang to any salad.

2 tsp	umeboshi paste
2 tbsp	tahini
2 tbsp	nutritional yeast flakes (page 15)
2 tbsp	flaxseed oil
1 tsp	kelp
	water to mix

Put everything in a small bowl, and blend together with a hand whisk. Add water drop by drop to reach desired consistency.

PER 15 g TABLESPOON	
Calories	65
Fat	5.9 g
Protein	2.1 g
Carbohydrate	1.0 g
Fiber	1.1 g

Nikki's Dressing

Yield: About one and a half cups

If your avocados are unripe, put them in a paper bag and leave them on the window sill to ripen them quickly. This works with most fruits.

Nikki first made this dressing for me and in doing so introduced me to the wonderful buttery flavor of flax oil. Flax oil adds depth and richness whenever it is used in a dish. It is very sensitive to heat and light, and can be found in the chiller cabinet of wholefood stores. Although it is expensive, it is an essential addition to your diet, being one of the few sources of essential fatty acids (the other main dietary source is fish).

¹/₂	avocado, mashed
1 tbsp	flaxseed oil
1 tbsp	Braggs Liquid Aminos (page 15)
1 tbsp	nutritional yeast flakes
1 tsp	kelp
1 tbsp	water

Put everything in a bowl, and blend together with a hand whisk.

PER 15 g TABLESPOON	
Calories	36
Fat	3.2 g
Protein	1.2 g
Carbohydrate	0.7 g
Fiber	0.8 g

PER 15 g TABLESPOON	
Calories	24
Fat	2.4 g
Protein	0.3 g
Carbohydrate	0.3 g
Fiber	0.4 g

PER 15 g TABLESPOON	
Calories	26
Fat	2.3 g
Protein	0.9 g
Carbohydrate	0.6 g
Fiber	0.3 g

Easy Avocado Mayo

This is an easy alternative to mayonnaise that you can knock up in a couple of minutes.

1	large avocado
2 tbsp	lemon juice
1 tsp	vinegar
1 tsp	tamari

Roughly chop the avocado. Put everything in the food processor, and blend for a few minutes until mixture thickens to the same consistency as egg mayonnaise.

Almond Mayo

This takes slightly longer to prepare than the previous recipe, but is more authentic.

4 oz	almond butter (page 34)
8 fl oz	water
1 fl oz	lemon juice
1 tsp	tamari
1	onion, chopped
1 tbsp	vinegar

Put everything in the blender, and process for a few minutes until the mixture thickens to the same consistency as egg mayonnaise.

It will thicken further when stored in the refrigerator.

Satay Sauce

This is a fantastic sauce; I particularly like it as a dip for broccoli and mushroom, or you can use it as a dip for Spring Rolls (page 60). Satay sauce is traditionally made from peanuts, but peanuts are not healthy for a number of reasons: they are extremely hard on the digestion, and are prone to a potentially carcinogenic fungus.

I always use fresh chilies in preference to chili powder. They have more flavor than the dried powder. Remove the seeds, because these are what cause your mouth to burn. If you prefer to use dried chili powder, one-fourth of a fresh chili is roughly equivalent to a half teaspoon of chili powder.

2 oz	dates
4 oz	almond butter (page 34)
I	red chili, finely chopped
I tbsp	tamari
	juice I lemon
2 tbsp	water

Break down the dates in the food processor until they form a homogenized mass. Add the nut butter and chili, and process until you have a paste. Lastly, add the tamari, lemon juice, and water, and purée until creamy.

PER 15 g TABLESPOON	
Calories	45
Fat	3.7 g
Protein	1.5 g
Carbohydrate	1.6 g
Fiber	0.5 g

Yield: About one and a half cups

If you are feeling adventurous, try mixing miso and molasses to make a nutritious spread for crackers such as Raw-Vita (page 57). The saltiness of the miso and the sweetness of the molasses offset each other to create an intriguing taste.

PER 15 g TABLESPOON	
Calories	9
Fat	0.1 g
Protein	0.3 g
Carbohydrate	1.7 g
Fiber	0.1 g

Yield: About one and a half cups

"Vegetables" that are horticulturally defined as fruits include cucumbers, peppers, tomatoes, zucchinis, eggplants, marrow, avocados and olives.

PER 15 g TABLESPOON	
Calories	232
Fat	13.0 g
Carbohydrate	25.2 g
Fiber	6.0 g

Barbeque Sauce

Use as a dip, a dressing, or a sauce for burgers.

6	tomatoes
3 tbsp	miso
4 tbsp	molasses
2	red chili, finely chopped

Roughly chop the tomatoes. Put everything in the food processor, and blend until smooth.

Salsa

Most people are familiar with salsa as a dip; it's actually Spanish for sauce. When it's freshly made, it's first rate, and makes a delightful salad in its own right.

	small bunch coriander
$1/2$	onion
$1/2$	red chili
	juice $1/2$ lemon
1 tsp	miso
1 tbsp	extra virgin olive oil
1 tsp	apple concentrate
6	tomatoes, cubed

In the food processor, blend thoroughly all ingredients apart from tomatoes. Add the tomatoes, process for a few seconds only, or by hand, so that they are thoroughly incorporated into the mixture but still retain their chunkiness.

Pasta Sauce

Yield: About three cups

I make this regularly for the children, omitting the garlic and chili. They love pasta, and I am happy for them to have it because I drown it in this nutritious sauce! I try to avoid wheat pasta and recently there has been a proliferation of excellent wheat-free pastas in the wholefood stores, made from grains such as corn, buckwheat, and rice.

This is currently the children's favorite dinner, and mine too! I don't eat cooked pasta, but either just eat the sauce as it is, as a dip for raw vegetables, or make raw "pasta" by peeling vegetables such as carrot and zucchini with a vegetable peeler. You can also buy a piece of equipment called a spiral slicer especially for this purpose.

6	tomatoes
1	avocado
3	carrots
2	stick celery
2 oz	dried tomatoes
8	dates
$1/2$	onion
4 tbsp	extra virgin olive oil
2 tbsp	tamari
2 tsp	vinegar
4 tbsp	fresh basil
2	clove garlic
1	red chili

Roughly chop the tomatoes, avocado, carrots, and celery. Put everything in the blender and blend to a thick sauce.

PER 15 g TABLESPOON	
Calories	626
Fat	37.4 g
Protein	10.5 g
Carbohydrate	66.1 g
Fiber	11.7 g

Tahini and Miso Gravy

Serve over burgers or nut loaf, or use as a dressing or dip. This has a rich, almost alcoholic flavor.

2 tbsp	tahini
1 tbsp	miso
2 tbsp	tamari
2 tbsp	extra virgin olive oil
4	dates
$^{1}/_{2}$	onion
2 tbsp	water
1	tomato

Put everything in the blender and purée until you get a thick sauce.

Yield: About one cup

If you can find a plentiful and inexpensive supply, use fresh dates in my recipes in preference to dried dates, which may not be raw, and often have less flavor. If you're using dried dates you may have to soak them for twenty minutes to an hour to soften them up. Drink the soaking water— it is delightfully sweet, and full of nutrients.

PER 15 g TABLESPOON	
Calories	23
Fat	1.6 g
Protein	0.4 g
Carbohydrate	1.8 g
Fiber	0.2 g

Yield: About a half cup

The cashews that we commonly come across are never raw, as they are heated to remove the shell. You can get raw ones, but they are less common.

PER 15 g TABLESPOON	
Calories	72
Fat	5.0 g
Protein	3.8 g
Carbohydrate	3.0 g
Fiber	1.7 g

Yield: About a half cup

I adore this. It has exactly the same sort of elasticity as melted cheese.

PER 15 g TABLESPOON	
Calories	48
Fat	2.7 g
Protein	2.7 g
Carbohydrate	3.6 g
Fiber	2.6 g
Contains at least 25% of the RDA for: Folate	

Grated "Cheese"

Serve sprinkled over a pasta dish, as a garnish for soup, or use to liven up a salad.

2 oz	cashew nuts
2 tbsp	nutritional yeast flakes
1 tbsp	nori flakes

Break cashews down in a grinder or a food processor until the pieces are small lumps the size of grated cheese. By hand, mix the nuts with the flakes, until they are thoroughly coated. A drop or two of water may help the flakes to stick.

Melted "Cheese"

What I love about these recipes is that their starting point is healthy, nutritious ingredients. But they end up tasting so yummy, that you want to eat them just for their fantastic flavors, and the nutritional value becomes secondary. For pizzas, or spread on crackers.

2 oz	ground flaxseed
2 tbsp	nutritional yeast flakes
1 tbsp	tamari
2 tbsp	water

Using a spoon, mix everything together, adding water gradually to make a thick paste. It will thicken further when stored; you may want to add more water to make it runnier.

4. Snacks and Side Dishes

Garlic Crackers

Pizza Crackers

Dulse Crackers

Hummus Crackers

Raw-Vita

Tomato Chips

"Roasted" Nuts

Spring Rolls

Stuffed Mushrooms

"Cheesy" Stuffed Peppers

Dill-Stuffed Peppers

Stuffed Avocado

Falafel

Onion Bhajis

Curried Spinach

Marinated Mushrooms

"Cooked" Buckwheat

Garlic Crackers

Yield: About twenty-five crackers

For nori crackers, replace parsley with two tablespoons nori flakes. Savory crackers are unbeatable spread with avocado and smothered in alfalfa. Or try any of the dips from the first section, topped with a selection of lettuce, tomato, alfalfa, etc.

If you are making crackers in the dehydrator, you need to cover the mesh trays with something to stop the mixture from sticking. Most kitchenware stores sell Teflon-coated sheets, specially designed for this purpose, or you can buy similar sheets in the supermarket and cut them to size.

10 oz	buckwheat, sprouted (page 13)
2 tbsp	cashews, ground
2 tbsp	flaxseed, ground
4	cloves garlic
1 tbsp	tamari
	small bunch parsley
2 tbsp	nutritional yeast flakes
2 tbsp	water

Put everything except the water in the food processor. Process for a couple of minutes until all the ingredients have formed a thick batter. Keep the machine on, and add water gradually, processing for another minute. Then spread into thin cracker shapes around three to four inches in diameter, and dehydrate for about twelve hours.

PER CRACKER

Calories	41
Fat	1.2 g
Carbohydrate	6.3 g
Fiber	0.7 g

Pizza Crackers

You can make this into two large rounds instead of individual crackers and use as pizza bases.

Most dehydrator crackers keep indefinitely if stored in an airtight container. The recipes here make quite large amounts for this reason, but if you discover a recipe you really love, it is worth doubling or even tripling the ingredients and making a really big batch at once.

6 oz	sprouted wheat (page 13)
large handful	fresh herbs—basil, rosemary, parsley, thyme, oregano
4	cloves garlic
4	tomatoes
2 tbsp	nutritional yeast flakes
I tbsp	tamari
2 tbsp	extra virgin olive oil

PER CRACKER

Calories	29
Fat	1.1 g
Carbohydrate	4.0 g
Fiber	0.4 g

Mash the sprouted wheat grain in the food processor (it won't break down completely). Add the herbs and garlic, and process until they are thoroughly mixed in. Next, add the tomatoes and blend them in. Then add the remaining ingredients and process for a minute more, until you have a thick batter. On dehydrator sheets, spread the batter into thin cracker shapes around three to four inches in diameter, and dehydrate for about twelve hours.

Dulse Crackers

These crackers are as delicious as they are nutritious. All of the crackers in this section benefit from being turned over, roughly two-thirds of the way through the dehydrating time, in order to achieve crispness on both sides.

4 oz	oat groats, soaked overnight
1 oz	dulse, rinsed
1	onion, roughly chopped
1 tbsp	miso
8 fl oz	water

Put everything in the blender, and purée until you have a thick batter. On dehydrator sheets, spread the batter into thin cracker shapes around three to four inches in diameter, and dehydrate for about twelve hours.

Hummus Crackers

We eat a lot of hummus, so I hit upon the idea of dehydrating it into crackers so we could enjoy it even more often.

	Raw Hummus (page 39)
1 ¹/₂	carrots
1	stick celery
2 tbsp	parsley
4 fl oz	water

Put everything in the blender, and purée until you have a thick batter. On dehydrator trays, spread the batter into thin crackers around three to four inches in diameter, and dehydrate for twelve hours.

Yield: About twenty large crackers

Rye reputedly helps with weight loss, hence its use in the slimming cracker.

Raw-Vita

Before I got my dehydrator, I would often supplement my salad with crackers and rice cakes. It was so gratifying to be able to make my own raw versions, just as pleasantly filling as the originals. These are a worthwhile base for any topping, sweet or savory.

5 oz	rye, soaked 10–12 hours, sprouted 3 days
2 oz	flaxseed, ground
1 tbsp	tamari
8 fl oz	water

Put everything in the blender, and purée until you have a thick batter. On dehydrator trays, spread the batter into thin, large, rectangular crackers, about five and a half inches by three inches and dehydrate for about twelve hours.

PER CRACKER	
Calories	41
Fat	1.2 g
Carbohydrate	6.8 g
Fiber	1.7 g

Yield: One small bag

These are addictive—
like a certain brand of
chips that comes in a
tube, once you start,
you can't stop!
Experiment with
different flavors: I
particularly like a
tablespoon of nori
flakes added to the
blended tomatoes, but
all herbs and spices
work well, or try a
tablespoon of tamari
and a tablespoon of
apple cider vinegar.

PER SERVING	
Calories	53
Fat	0.3 g
Protein	2.7 g
Carbohydrate	10.5 g
Fiber	1.5 g

Tomato Chips

*Dried tomatoes possess an incredibly intense sweetness which adds
depth to a dish. In this recipe, they make delightful chips that are a
wonderful alternative to potato chips, and go well with dips such as
hummus and guacamole. For a decent-sized bag of chips, multiply
the recipe by three.*

5	tomatoes

Put tomatoes in food processor and purée until they are a
soupy mixture, with no lumps left. Carefully pour onto a
dehydrator tray, spreading as thinly as possible. Dehydrate
for twelve to eighteen hours, until completely dry and crisp.

The length of time varies greatly between different
varieties of tomato—the more watery the tomato, the longer it
will take. Fleshier tomatoes work better and have more flavor.
When done, remove the sheet, and snap into chip-sized
pieces. Store in a sealed plastic bag for your very own packet
of raw chips! Larger pieces make good wrappers for Roll-Ups
(page 86).

"Roasted" Nuts

These are a staple in our house. We eat them daily—a big reason to invest in a dehydrator! We eat them as snacks, or add them to savory dishes where nuts are required, for extra flavor. They take on the salty, crunchy qualities of roasted nuts without the unhealthy effects of refined salt and heated oils.

Yield: About three pounds

1 lb	walnuts
1 lb	cashews
8 oz	sunflower seeds
8 oz	pumpkin seeds
5 pints	shoyu (or tamari)

Soak the nuts and seeds for twelve hours in pure water. At the end of this time, drain off the water, and marinate in shoyu for twenty-four hours. When done, drain off the shoyu, and dehydrate for twenty-four hours. They keep indefinitely, stored in airtight containers.

The shoyu can be reused three to four times for marinating. It may develop harmless white yeasts, which you should remove. When it starts to smell, throw it away!

PER 15 g TABLESPOON	
Calories	97
Fat	8.2 g
Protein	3.2 g
Carbohydrate	2.8 g
Fiber	0.7 g

Yield: Makes six rolls

The following recipes in this section make sensational starters or combine with a side salad to make a complete meal. For a Chinese style meal, have Spring Rolls and Satay Sauce (page 48) as a starter, followed by Sweet and Sour (page 98) for the main course.

PER ROLL

Calories	64
Fat	4.1 g
Carbohydrate	5.7 g
Fiber	1.5 g

Contains at least 25% of the RDA for: Vitamins C and A

Spring Rolls

You can grow your own mung bean sprouts, or buy standard beansprouts. These are specially grown to make them long and straight, and bear little outward similarity to homegrown sprouts! Homegrown ones are more nutritious, while store-bought ones make a more authentic dish.

2	cloves garlic
	small bunch parsley
$1/_2$ inch	piece fresh ginger
$1/_4$	onion
3 oz	cabbage
1	carrot
$1/_2$	red pepper
3 oz	mung bean sprouts (page 13)
1 tbsp	tamari
1 tbsp	apple cider vinegar
1 tbsp	apple concentrate
2 tbsp	sesame oil
6	large Romaine lettuce leaves

In the food processor, mash the garlic, parsley, ginger, and onion. Next, grate the cabbage, carrot, and red pepper. Transfer everything (apart from the lettuce leaves) to a mixing bowl, and stir thoroughly, until evenly mixed. When the filling is ready, take the lettuce leaves, spread them out on a plate, and place a few spoons of the filling on each leaf, making sure you divide it evenly between the leaves. With a knife or the back of a spoon, spread the filling across the leaf, covering it all. Finally, roll the leaf tightly from top to bottom (but not too tightly or the filling will splurge out the sides).

Stuffed Mushrooms

If, like me, you love olives, this is an excuse to eat lots of them! Olives and mushrooms are a gorgeous earthy combination.

Olives have the highest mineral count of any fruit, and are also abundant in amino acids, essential fatty acids, and antioxidants.

6¹/₂ oz	pitted black olives
I oz	dried tomatoes
I¹/₂	carrots, chopped
I	stick celery, chopped
2 tbsp	fresh parsley
2 tbsp	fresh basil
2	cloves garlic
2 tbsp	flax seed, ground
2 tbsp	tahini
2	portobello (flat) mushrooms

Put everything apart from the mushrooms in the food processor, and process down to a smooth purée. Cover the underside of the mushrooms with this mixture. If you are able, dehydrate for about four hours before serving.

PER SERVING

Calories	342
Fat	26.0 g
Carbohydrate	16.9 g
Fiber	12.3 g

Contains at least 25% of the RDA for: Iron, Calcium, Vitamins B1, B2, B3, B6, Folate, Vitamins C, A and E

"Cheesy" Stuffed Peppers

Yield: Serves two

I adore stuffed peppers—almost any combination of nuts and vegetables tastes fantastic in that crispy red or yellow shell. However, this has got to be the best filling I've made —it's unbelievably cheesy!

One ear of corn has approximately 800 kernels arranged in 16 rows. Fresh corn on the cob makes a great raw snack—juicy and refreshing, just eat it as it is.

13 oz	corn kernels (approximately 4 cobs)
$1^1/_2$	carrots, chopped
	small bunch parsley, chopped
2 tbsp	ground flaxseed
2 tbsp	extra virgin olive oil
1 tsp	miso
2 tbsp	nutritional yeast flakes
$^1/_2$	red chili
2	cloves garlic
$^1/_2$	onion
4 fl oz	orange juice
2	large red peppers

PER SERVING

Calories	516
Fat	21.5 g
Carbohydrate	66.4 g
Fiber	14.1 g

Contains at least 25% of the RDA for: Iron, Vitamins B1, B2, B3, B6, Folate, Vitamins C, A and E

Put everything apart from the peppers and orange juice in the blender. Purée, adding orange juice gradually until the mixture is completely blended. Don't use all the juice if you don't have to: you want the mixture to be as thick as possible, but without lumps. Next, slice the peppers in half lengthwise and remove the stalk and seeds. Then fill the peppers with the cheese mixture. If possible, dehydrate for six hours.

Dill-stuffed Peppers

Yield: Serves three

Red peppers are sweeter and more flavorful than their green counterparts, as well as containing nine times more Vitamin A and twice as much Vitamin C.

PER SERVING

Calories	147
Fat	6.8 g
Carbohydrate	17.7 g
Fiber	4.6 g

Contains at least 25% of the RDA for: Vitamins B6, Folate, Vitamins C, A and E

You can also make this using pumpkin seeds instead of sunflower seeds. Use four ounces of pumpkin seeds, and soak them overnight first. Pumpkin seeds are a very good source of zinc.

2 oz	sprouted sunflower seeds (page 13)
2 tbsp	tahini
1	large carrot, chopped
1	stick celery, chopped
1/4	onion
	small bunch dill
1 tbsp	tamari
2 tbsp	lemon juice
3	red peppers

Put the sunflower seeds, tahini, carrot, celery, onion, and dill in the food processor, and process until they are thoroughly blended. Add the tamari and lemon juice, and mix again so you have a thick purée. Next, slice the peppers in half lengthwise and remove the stalk and seeds. Then stuff the peppers with the sunflower mixture and, if possible, dehydrate for four hours.

Stuffed Avocado

Perfect as a starter. "Roasted" Nuts (page 59) work well in this dish.

(page 59)

2 oz	sunflower and/or pumpkin seeds
1	carrot, chopped
2 tbsp	dried tomatoes
1 tsp	miso
1 tbsp	nutritional yeast flakes
$^1/_2$	onion
$^1/_4$	red chili
$^1/_2$ oz	fresh basil leaves
1 oz	alfalfa sprouts
2	small avocados

Put everything apart from the alfalfa and avocados in the food processor. Process for a couple of minutes until you have a thick purée. Next, slice the avocados in half and remove the stones. Then fill the holes where the stones were with the mixture, and cover the flesh with a thin layer. Top with alfalfa sprouts, covering each half, and serve on a bed of lettuce.

Yield: Serves two as a main dish, or four as a side dish.

I love avocados just as they are: I simply halve them, remove the stone, sprinkle with a little sea salt, and scoop out the flesh from the shell with a spoon; for some reason, when eaten this way they are reminiscent of boiled eggs.

PER SERVING

Calories	430
Fat	32.8 g
Carbohydrate	21.1 g
Fiber	8.1 g

Contains at least 25% of the RDA for: Iron, Vitamins B1, B2, B6, Folate, Vitamins A and E

Falafel

Falafel is a Middle Eastern dish, traditionally served with salad and hummus in pita bread. These taste divine on their own, or try using lettuce or Chinese leaves in place of the pita, and fill with Raw Hummus (page 39), alfalfa, lettuce, and tomato for a complete meal.

8 oz	chick peas, sprouted (page 13)
5 oz	tahini
4 fl oz	extra virgin olive oil
1 tbsp	tamari
4 fl oz	lemon juice
bunch	fresh coriander
4	cloves garlic
1	medium onion
2 tsp	ground cumin

Put everything in the blender, and purée for a few minutes until the mixture is a smooth batter. Place tablespoons of the mixture onto a dehydrating sheet, about one inch high. Dehydrate for about ten hours.

Yield: About twenty falafels

These are tricky to make without a dehydrator. You can try making them in the food processor instead. Use less extra virgin olive oil, tamari and lemon juice, so the mixture is less liquid and sticks together more. Then roll them into balls by hand.

PER FALAFEL

Calories	119
Fat	10.3 g
Carbohydrate	3.9 g
Fiber	1.2g

Onion Bhajis

Yield: About ten Bhajis

You can use any vegetable in place of the onion—try broccoli, cauliflower, spinach, or pea bhajis. Or double the quantities and make mixed veggie bhajis.

Like the falafel, I feel that these are superior to their cooked counterparts—not so fatty and starchy.

1–2 oz	onion
8 oz	chick pea sprouts (page 13)
2 tbsp	extra virgin olive oil
1 tbsp	tamari
2 tbsp	water
$1/2$	red chili
$1/2$ tsp	ground cumin
1	clove garlic
1 tbsp	garam masala

Finely chop the onion, or whichever vegetable you are using. Put all the other ingredients in the blender and purée until you have a smooth batter. Stir in the chopped onion (or vegetables) with a spoon. Form into patty shapes about one inch high, and dehydrate for about ten hours.

PER BHAJI

Calories	59
Fat	2.6 g
Carbohydrate	6.7 g
Fiber	1.0 g

Curried Spinach

One of my favorite Indian dishes was Sag Aloo, which is curried spinach and potatoes. This is my raw version—I sometimes add a few chopped boiled potatoes to make it more authentic.

8 oz	spinach or chard
2 tsp	miso
2 tsp	tahini
2 tsp	garam masala
$1/2$	onion
$1/2$	red chili, finely chopped

Break down spinach in food processor for a couple of minutes, until it is a thick paste. Add the remaining ingredients and process briefly until they are blended in.

Yield: Serves two

Serve with Spicy Carrot and Apple Salad (page 70) and Onion Bhajis (page 66) for a complete Indian meal.

PER SERVING

Calories	102
Fat	5.1 g
Carbohydrate	7.9 g
Fiber	3.4 g

Contains at least 25% of the RDA for: Iron, Calcium, Folate, Vitamins C and A

Yield: Serves two

You can keep these in the refrigerator, and add a few to salads. They make a lovely alternative to fried mushrooms. Be careful to drain off all the excess marinade, so that they're not too greasy.

PER SERVING	
Calories	222
Fat	21.0 g
Carbohydrate	3.8 g
Fiber	2.2 g

Contains at least 25% of the RDA for: Vitamins B2, B3 and Folate

Yield: Serves two

You can turn this into a complete meal by adding grated vegetables such as carrots and chopped herbs and seasonings such as miso and garlic to the thermos.

PER SERVING	
Calories	251
Fat	1.6 g
Carbohydrate	53.2 g
Fiber	1.4 g

Marinated Mushrooms

Crimini mushrooms are very small button mushrooms. If you can't get them, use chestnut mushrooms and slice about one-quarter inch thick.

8 tbsp	extra virgin olive oil
16 fl oz	tamari
13 oz	crimini mushrooms
8	cloves garlic, crushed

Put the mushrooms and garlic in a large bowl, and pour the olive oil and tamari over them. Keep in the refrigerator for eight to twelve hours, stirring intermittently. At the end of this time, drain and serve.

"Cooked" Buckwheat

Gratifying in the winter when you fancy something hot. You can try this with any sprout. I like quinoa.

8 oz	sprouted buckwheat (page 13)
2 pint	boiled water

Place buckwheat and water in a thermos flask, and screw the lid on. Leave for twenty-four hours. When done, spoon out of the flask, and serve with Tahini and Miso Gravy (page 51). Eat it immediately, and it will still taste warm and cooked.

5. Salads

SIDE SALADS

Apple Salad	*Beet Salad*
Spicy Carrot and Apple Salad	*Carrot Cake Salad*
Apple and Olive Salad	*Pad Thai*
Coleslaw	*Cauliflower Cheese*
Eat Your Greens	*Lentil and Watercress Salad*
Cucumbers and Ketchup	*Chris's Lunch*
Sweet Greens	*Miso Mushrooms*
Celeriac Salad	

MAIN COURSE SALADS

Basic Salad	*Almond, Avocado, and Mushroom Salad*
Pesto Salad	*Thai Green Papaya Salad*
Sauerkraut Salad	*Chris's Salad*

Yield: Serves two

I always use fresh coconut, but desiccated is an acceptable alternative. If you prefer, you can use unpasteurized honey instead of rice syrup.

PER SERVING	
Calories	405
Fat	14.8 g
Carbohydrate	66.5 g
Fiber	7.5 g

Yield: Serves two

PER SERVING	
Calories	357
Fat	10.1 g
Carbohydrate	59.5 g
Fiber	13.4g

Apple Salad

A sweet salad. Serve as a snack, or as an accompaniment to spicy dishes.

4	grated apples
4 tbsp	raisins
4 tbsp	dates
4 tbsp	grated fresh coconut
2 tsp	Almond Butter (page 34)
2 tsp	rice syrup
I tsp	Chinese 5-spice (page 15)

Toss all the ingredients together and serve immediately.

Spicy Carrot and Apple Salad

This salad is an interesting mix of sweet and sour.

16 oz	grated carrot
16 oz	grated apple
2 tbsp	nutritional yeast flakes
2 tbsp	"Roasted" Nuts (page 59)
I tsp	hot chili sauce

Toss all ingredients together and serve immediately.

Yield: Serves two

It is difficult to be sure that you are buying raw olives. Canned ones are pasteurized, and are best avoided. The best ones to buy are sun-ripened black olives, if you can find them.

PER SERVING	
Calories	235
Fat	14.8 g
Carbohydrate	19.3 g
Fiber	7.4 g

Contains at least 25% of the RDA for: Folate and Vitamin E

Yield: Serves two

We use hemp seeds as they add a lovely crunch to this dish, but you could use pine nuts, sesame seeds, or walnuts.

PER SERVING	
Calories	306
Fat	17.4 g
Carbohydrate	31.4 g
Fiber	12.6 g

Contains at least 25% of the RDA for: Vitamins B1, B6, Folate, Vitamins C, A and E

Apple and Olive Salad

Olives are a fruit, and so combine surprisingly well with apples. You can also try substituting apples with oranges in this recipe: use two oranges, peeled and chopped.

8 oz	apple, grated
6	lettuce leaves, shredded
5 oz	pitted olives
2 tbsp	nutritional yeast flakes
2 tsp	flax oil
2 tsp	Braggs Liquid Aminos (page 15)

Toss all ingredients together and serve.

Coleslaw

This is the basic coleslaw recipe, but experiment with it. For example, you could use red cabbage, or replace the carrot with beet or apple. The amount of mayonnaise you use will depend on its viscosity—thicker mayonnaise will coat the vegetables better.

4	carrots
13 oz	white cabbage
1	onion
2 tbsp	hemp seeds
3–4 tbsp	mayonnaise (page 47)
	freshly ground sea salt and black pepper

Grate carrot, cabbage, and onion. Then toss with remaining ingredients. Add salt and pepper.

Yield: Serves two

I've used spinach, kale, chard, green cabbage, bok choy, arugala, lettuce, and celery in this dish. It also provides a welcome use for leftover broccoli stems.

PER SERVING	
Calories	208
Fat	14.7 g
Carbohydrate	9.6 g
Fiber	10.9 g

Contains at least 25% of the RDA for: Iron, Vitamins B2, B6, Folate, Vitamins C and A

Yield: Serves two

This is a popular salad with children—don't they love anything that's covered in ketchup?

PER SERVING	
Calories	89
Fat	1.0 g
Carbohydrate	16.9 g
Fiber	4.7 g

Contains at least 25% of the RDA for: Vitamin B6, Folate, Vitamins C, A and E

Eat Your Greens

This is one of our favorites. I make it nearly every week, as it is so nutritious. It comes out quite differently depending on what greens you use. Spinach and lettuce are quite runny, kale is rather chewy. Experiment with different combinations to see which you like best.

6–12 oz	greens
1	avocado
4	gherkins, chopped
2 tbsp	dulse
2 tbsp	nutritional yeast flakes
2 tsp	kelp

Put greens in food processor and process until they are evenly chopped with no large pieces remaining. Add avocado and process for half a minute, until it is completely mixed with the greens. Then add the remaining ingredients and process briefly until they are mixed in. The resulting mix should not be a purée, but still have some texture, with the individual ingredients discernible. Serve as a side salad to Burgers (page 87) or Nut Loaf (page 89).

Cucumbers and Ketchup

I don't think this would be quite the same with traditional ketchup!

1	cucumber, cubed
2	red pepper, cubed
4 tbsp	fresh dill, finely chopped
4 tbsp	Tomato Ketchup (page 43)

Toss all ingredients together.

Yield: Serves two

Fresh tamarind is hard to come across, but worth getting if you can. It has a similar taste to dates, and is a common ingredient in Indian chutneys and curries. If you can't find it, use dates instead.

PER SERVING	
Calories	301
Fat	16.6 g
Carbohydrate	28.8 g
Fiber	11 g

Contains at least 25% of the RDA for: Iron, Calcium, Vitamins B1, B2, Vitamins C and A

Yield: Serves two

Celeriac is an underused vegetable. If you're cooking, it's particularly appetizing when made into fries (page 159). It also goes well with Umeboshi Dressing (page 45).

PER SERVING	
Calories	106
Fat	5.4 g
Carbohydrate	9.1 g
Fiber	8.9 g

Contains at least 25% of the RDA for: Vitamin B1, Folate, and Vitamin C

Sweet Greens

This is another unusual combination that is surprisingly tasty.

6–12 oz	greens (page 72)
1	avocado
4 tbsp	fresh tamarind
2 tbsp	dulse
2 tbsp	garam masala

Put the greens in the food processor and break down to a mash. Add remaining ingredients and process for a minute until they are blended in.

Celeriac Salad

Shredded celeriac in a spicy mayonnaise sauce is a traditional Northern European dish.

1	celeriac, peeled and grated
4 tbsp	Almond Mayo (page 30)
8	cloves garlic, crushed

Toss all the ingredients together, and marinate in refrigerator for twelve to twenty-four hours, to soften the celeriac.

Yield: Serves two

Apples are one of the most popular fruits in the world, growing almost everywhere: there are around 40 million tons of apples produced every year. There are over three thousand varieties of apples!

PER SERVING

Calories	505
Fat	31.9 g
Carbohydrate	49.1 g
Fiber	10.4 g

Contains at least 25% of the RDA for: Iron, Folate, Vitamins C and E

Yield: Serves two

Carrots are the best source of carotene, which the body converts to vitamin A, and the second most popular vegetable in the world, after the potato.

PER SERVING

Calories	566
Fat	11.0 g
Carbohydrate	111.2 g
Fiber	8.4 g

Contains at least 25% of the RDA for: Iron, Calcium, Vitamins B1, B6, Folate and Vitamin A

Beet Salad

Choose smaller beetroots, which are sweeter than the larger ones. The leaves are mineral rich, and also edible; use like spinach.

16 oz	beet, peeled and grated
16 oz	apple, grated
4 tbsp	mayonnaise
2 tbsp	sesame seeds

Toss all ingredients together and serve.

Carrot Cake Salad

This is a very sweet salad, probably best served on its own, as a snack. It's a terrific one to serve children.

2 tbsp	tahini
2 tbsp	rice syrup
2 tsp	cinnamon
	water to mix
6	carrots, grated
8 tbsp	raisins
6 oz	wheat sprouts (page 13)

In a small bowl or teacup, mix tahini, rice syrup, cinnamon, and a little water to make a thick dressing. Then put the remaining ingredients in a larger bowl, and toss them in the dressing.

Pad Thai

My version of the classic noodle dish. The daikon radish acts as a substitute for noodles; if you can't get daikon radish, green papaya, Jerusalem artichokes, or even, in a pinch, white cabbage would do.

Yield: Serves two

Daikon radish, rather like a large white carrot in appearance, is also known as daikon, or Chinese radish. It is very cleansing and refreshing, with a slight bite to it.

4	lettuce leaves, shredded
4	Chinese leaves, shredded
12	cherry tomatoes, halved
2	daikon radish, grated
4	mushrooms, sliced
3 oz	green beans, chopped
3 oz	mung bean sprouts (page 13)
2	red chili, finely chopped
4	cloves garlic, crushed
2 tbsp	sesame oil
2 tbsp	apple concentrate
2 tbsp	tamari
4 tbsp	cashews, chopped

PER SERVING

Calories	374
Fat	26.6 g
Carbohydrate	24.6 g
Fiber	4.4 g

Contains at least 25% of the RDA for: Iron, Vitamins B1, B6, Folate and Vitamin C

With salad servers, mix the lettuce, Chinese leaf, and tomatoes. Arrange on a plate as a bed for the rest of the salad. Next, put the daikon radish, mushrooms, green beans, and bean sprouts in a bowl and mix together with the salad servers. Then add the chili, garlic, sesame oil, apple concentrate, and tamari to the vegetables, and toss.

Lastly, place this mixture on the lettuce bed, and sprinkle the cashews over the top.

Cauliflower Cheese

*If you want to impress guests, multiply this recipe by four, and use
a whole, intact cauliflower. Mark Twain famously claimed that
cauliflower is "nothing but a cabbage with a college education."*

20 oz	cauliflower, divided into bite-sized florets
8 oz	tahini
2 tsp	tamari
4 tbsp	water
4 tbsp	nutritional yeast flakes

Put all the ingredients except the cauliflower in a bowl and
blend together with a hand whisk. Pour over cauliflower,
toss, and serve.

Lentil and Watercress Salad

*Watercress is very health giving—packed full of minerals, particularly
iron and calcium, as well as being rich in Vitamins A and C.*

2 bunch	watercress
4 oz	lentil sprouts (page 13)
1	avocado, chopped
1 tsp	kelp
2 tbsp	plain live yogurt (page 15)

Using scissors, cut and discard the stems of the watercress,
and snip the rest into bite-sized pieces. Then put all
ingredients in a bowl and toss together.

Yield: Serves two

You can use discarded avocado stones to grow your own houseplants. Push the stone into soil, leaving the pointed end exposed. Keep warm until shoots appear.

PER SERVING	
Calories	470
Fat	38.0 g
Carbohydrate	22.1 g
Fiber	9.2 g

Contains at least 25% of the RDA for: Vitamins B1, B3, B6, Folate, Vitamins C, A and E

Yield: Serves two

If you can't get oyster mushrooms, chestnut mushrooms work just as well. As oyster mushrooms have a fairly robust flavor when eaten raw, you may want to mix half and half.

PER SERVING	
Calories	274
Fat	19.6 g
Carbohydrate	8.9 g
Fiber	4.8 g

Contains at least 25% of the RDA for: Iron, Calcium, Vitamins B1, B6 and Folate

Chris's Lunch

A simple favorite of my husband's. It makes a quick, scrumptious, satisfying lunch.

2	avocado, cubed
6	tomatoes, cubed
4 tbsp	"Roasted" Nuts (page 59)
1 tbsp	Braggs Liquid Aminos (page 15)
	freshly ground black pepper

Toss all ingredients together. Add pepper as needed.

Miso Mushrooms

This has a rich, decadent flavor.

2 tsp	miso
2 tbsp	nutritional yeast flakes
4 tbsp	tahini
4 tbsp	water
4	cloves garlic, minced
13 oz	oyster mushrooms

Using a hand whisk, beat together all the ingredients apart from the oyster mushrooms. Then slice the mushrooms into small pieces, and toss in the sauce.

Basic Salad

Yield: Serves two

This is my foolproof recipe for an unbeatable salad that can be adapted to whatever you have around the kitchen.

Don't forget about the many different varieties of salad leaves available—for example, Romaine, iceberg, arugala, frisee, radicchio, and endive.

6$^{1}/_{2}$ oz	leafy greens
10 oz	non-sweet fruit
5 oz	vegetables
1 oz	alfalfa sprouts (page 12)
2 oz	bean sprouts (page 13)
	seaweed
2 tbsp	pickles
1	avocado
2 tbsp	crunchy bits
	dressing

PER SERVING WITHOUT DRESSING

Calories	626
Fat	51.4 g
Carbohydrate	20.2 g
Fiber	17.4 g

Contains at least 25% of the RDA for: Iron, Zinc, Calcium, Vitamins B1, B2, B3, B6, Folate, Vitamins C, A and E

Start with two types of leafy greens, such as lettuce, spinach, watercress, bok choy, Chinese leaf, lambs leaf, or arugala.

Use three ounces of each. Don't rinse, and don't use a knife on them, as this makes them lose their crispness. If they need cleaning, wipe them with a kitchen towel. If you are using organic leaves, don't be fastidious—a bit of organic soil is good for you! Make sure that you check carefully for bugs. Tear the greens into small pieces; watercress may need chopping with scissors, leave small leaves such as lambs leaf whole.

Add five ounces each of two types of non-sweet fruit, such as tomatoes, cucumber, pepper, or mushroom. Then add a vegetable; our favorites are broccoli, cauliflower, celery, grated carrot, or grated beet. Put in some alfalfa sprouts, and more sprouts such as lentil, mung bean, or sunflower. Next add seaweed—two tablespoons dulse or arame, one tablespoon nori flakes, or one teaspoon kelp. Then you want some pickled vegetables like gherkins, pickled onions, or sauerkraut, and don't forget one avocado, cubed. Finally, add crunchy bits such as pine nuts, pumpkin seeds, hemp seeds, "Roasted" Nuts (page 59), or sesame seeds. Toss all ingredients together with salad servers.

Add your preferred dressing and serve immediately (dressings, pages 43–46). If you make a salad and leave it to stand, it will go limp and soggy. If you have to make it in advance, prepare all the ingredients apart from the leaves and the crunchy bits, and add these in at the very last minute.

Yield: Serves two

Choose chestnut mushrooms that have tightly closed caps; if the gills are showing, it means they are past their prime.

PER SERVING

Calories	272
Fat	23.8 g
Carbohydrate	7.5 g
Fiber	6.3 g

Contains at least 25% of the RDA for: Vitamin B6, Folate, Vitamins C, A and E

Pesto Salad

Pesto is a raw Italian basil paste traditionally added to pasta. You can make your own pesto, but you need a lot of basil and I've yet to find a worthwhile vegan recipe (conventional pesto is made with cheese). However, there are some pleasing vegan pestos in the shops, which we often use as salad dressing.

3	mushrooms
3	tomatoes
I	avocado
I tbsp	pesto
I tbsp	nutritional yeast flakes
I tbsp	pine nuts
2 tsp	nori flakes

Chop mushrooms, tomatoes, and avocado into equal bite-sized chunks. Place in a bowl and toss with the remaining ingredients.

Sauerkraut Salad

Yield: Serves two

You can make your own sauerkraut at home very simply and cheaply by fermenting grated cabbage with sea salt or sea vegetables. Alternatively, it is quite easy to find it in health food stores. Look for jars that say they are unpasteurized; this should mean they are raw.

Sauerkraut is cabbage that has been grated and allowed to ferment. A traditional German dish, it is full of enzymes and beneficial bacteria, and is wonderful for the digestion.

6^1/$_2$ oz	lettuce leaves, torn
6^1/$_2$ oz	spinach leaves, torn
1	avocado, diced
3	tomatoes, diced
8 oz	sauerkraut
1 oz	dulse, rinsed
1 oz	alfalfa sprouts (page 12)
1 tsp	kelp
1 tbsp	nutritional yeast flakes
	dash Braggs Liquid Aminos (page 15)
	dash sesame oil

Toss all ingredients together.

PER SERVING

Calories	234
Fat	17.2 g
Carbohydrate	9.2 g
Fiber	13.1 g

Contains at least 25% of the RDA for: Iron, Calcium, Vitamins B1, B2, B6, Folate, Vitamins C, A and E

Almond, Avocado, and Mushroom Salad

Yield: Serves two

Tofu isn't a raw food. It is made from cooked, pressed soybeans. It is high in protein and calcium, and originates from Japan. Once touted as an essential part of the vegetarian diet, soy is now experiencing something of a backlash. Ultimately, too much of any processed food is never advantageous, and soy does tend to be heavily processed before it reaches our plates, so I don't eat it too often.

This is a hearty, high-protein salad.

$6^{1}/_{2}$ oz	lettuce, torn
I bunch	watercress, chopped
4 oz	almonds or cubed tofu
$^{1}/_{2}$	avocado, chopped
2 tbsp	dulse, rinsed and torn
$3^{1}/_{2}$ oz	oyster mushroom, shredded
I oz	alfalfa sprouts (page 12)
60 g	cherry tomatoes, halved
2 tbsp	olives, pitted

Toss everything together. Serve with a thick creamy dressing such as Miso-Mayo Dressing (page 43) or Ultimate Dressing (page 44).

PER SERVING

Calories	1008
Fat	89.5 g
Carbohydrate	15.6 g
Fiber	21.0 g

Contains at least 25% of the RDA for: Iron, Zinc, Calcium, Vitamins B1, B2, B3, B6, Folate, Vitamins C, A and E

Thai Green Papaya Salad

This is one of the most popular Thai salads. You can substitute green mango for the green papaya. These are simply unripe fruit, in which the starches have not turned to sugars, so they are not sweet.

In Thailand, they serve this with a lot more chili—beware if you order it in a Thai restaurant! If you do overheat, don't try drinking water, as this makes the burning worse. Eat some ice cream, yogurt or lassi (page 149)—something cold and creamy.

1	green papaya, peeled and grated
3 oz	green beans, chopped
4 tbsp	mung bean sprouts (page 13)
4 tbsp	chopped cashews

DRESSING

2	large tomato
6	cloves garlic
2	red chili
2 tbsp	tamari
2 tbsp	apple concentrate
	juice 1 lemon

Toss all salad ingredients together. Blend dressing ingredients together in food processor until they form a smooth purée—be especially careful not to leave any lumps of garlic or chili! Toss salad in dressing.

PER SERVING

Calories	307
Fat	15.5 g
Carbohydrate	32.8 g
Fiber	6.5 g

Contains at least 25% of the RDA for: Iron, Vitamins B1, B6, Folate, Vitamins C and E

Chris's Salad

The secret is in the dressing. Toasted sesame oil is not raw, but a few drops add incredible flavor to a dish.

Yield: Serves two

My husband, a creature of habit, invariably makes himself this whenever I am having a night off from the kitchen. He has made it so many times that he has perfected the balance of the ingredients, and we both agree that this is the best salad we have ever eaten.

6¹/₂ oz	mixed leaves, e.g. lettuces, lambs leaf, watercress, baby spinach, arugala
¹/₄	red pepper
1	mushroom
1	tomato
2	gherkins
3	marinated sun-dried tomatoes
1	small head broccoli
1 tbsp	dulse
1	avocado
2 tbsp	sprouts (whatever you have on hand—pages 12–13)
10	pitted olives
2 tbsp	pine kernels
2 tbsp	alfalfa sprouts (page 12)
2 tbsp	"Roasted" Nuts (page 59)
2 tbsp	nutritional yeast flakes
¹/₂ tsp	kelp
¹/₂ tbsp	Braggs Liquid Aminos (page 15)
1 tsp	sesame oil
1 tbsp	pickle

PER SERVING

Calories	948
Fat	72.3 g
Carbohydrate	38.1 g
Fiber	26.2 g

Contains at least 25% of the RDA for: Iron, Zinc, Calcium, Vitamins B1, B2, B3, B6, Folate, Vitamins C, A and E

Chop red pepper, mushrooms, tomatoes, gherkins, sun-dried tomatoes, broccoli, dulse, and avocado, small enough so that you can get a variety of ingredients on your fork. In a large bowl, toss together so that all the ingredients are evenly distributed. Then add the sprouts, olives, pine kernels, alfalfa, "Roasted" Nuts (page 59), nutritional yeast, and kelp, and toss again. Next, tear the leaves and add them in. Finally add the Braggs, sesame oil, and pickle (which is not a raw food), and toss once more. Serve immediately.

6. Main Courses

Roll-Ups or Wraps

BURGERS

Brazil Nut Burgers

Mushroom Burgers

Nut Loaf

Sunflower Sausages

Creamy Calcium Vegetables

Dolmades

Sprouted Tabbouleh

Ratatouille

Corn Supreme

Pizza

Winter Vegetable Stew

Sweet and Sour

Thai Green Curry

Almond Curry

Coconut Curry

Tomato and Asparagus Curry

Roll-Ups or Wraps

There is no limit to the different combinations of Roll-Ups you can create. Basically, you take a leaf, spread it with your favorite spread, stuff with some sprouts or vegetables, roll, and serve. I invariably make this once a week because it is so easy but so gorgeous! Here are a few of my favorite combinations.

CARROT Carole's Carrot Dip (page 35) on lettuce leaves, cover in alfalfa

GUACAMOLE Guacamole (page 37) on Chinese leaf, cover with alfalfa and mung bean sprouts

RED HOT PEPPER ROLLS Red Hot Pepper Dip (page 38) on cabbage leaves, cover with lentil sprouts, alfalfa, cucumber and tomato

SPICY Mayonnaise (page 47) and hot chili sauce on lettuce leaves, cover with cucumber, tomato, mushroom, and lots of mung bean sprouts

SUNFLOWER ROLLS Sunflower Pâté (page 40) and alfalfa in Chinese leaf

NORI I Avocado, mushroom, tomato, red chili, and bean sprouts rolled in a nori sheet

NORI II Cucumber, tofu, spring onion, and alfalfa rolled in a nori sheet

Lettuce leaves work best because they are thin and roll easily. Chinese leaf, bok choy, and large spinach leaves all make respectable rolls. I like white and red cabbage, but they are a bit tougher to chew. Nori sheets are traditionally used in sushi making. If you buy the untoasted variety, they are raw. You can also use large pieces of Tomato Chips (page 58) but you need to eat these wraps immediately as the tomato "wrapper" goes soggy.

Yield: Makes eight burgers

Don't attempt to omit the flaxseeds from this recipe, as they are the binding agent. Flaxseeds behave differently from other seeds. You cannot eat them raw; the easiest way to consume them is by grinding them up and adding them to food. If you soak them for a few hours (not longer), they swell up and form a sticky mass. You can eat them this way if you choose but they are not very palatable!

PER BURGER

Calories	277
Fat	24.1 g
Carbohydrate	8.0 g
Fiber	4.9 g

Contains at least 25% of the RDA for: Folate, Vitamins A and E

Burgers

All burgers are fantastic served on a Chinese leaf folded round to make a bun, with mayonnaise, ketchup, alfalfa, gherkins, and a slice of tomato inside. If you want to go the whole way, serve with Coleslaw (page 71), The Best Fries (page 159) and a Smoothie (page 153). If you don't have a dehydrator, omit the water in the recipe, and eat raw or grill lightly.

Brazil Nut Burgers

4	sticks celery
3	carrots
I	onion
	small bunch parsley
8 oz	brazil nuts
2 oz	flaxseed, ground
2 tbsp	nutritional yeast flakes
I tbsp	tamari
4 oz	water

Roughly chop the celery, carrots, onion, and parsley. Put them in the food processor with the nuts, and process until all the ingredients are blended together. Then add the remaining ingredients, and process again to make a thick paste. On a dehydrator tray, shape into burgers about one-half inch thick, and dehydrate for seven hours.

Mushroom Burgers

Mushrooms are neither a fruit nor a vegetable, but a fungus, in a classification of their own. Both the ancient Chinese and the Romans viewed mushrooms as a food of the gods, and would give them as a divine offering.

Mushrooms contain protein, minerals, and B vitamins, and are rich in polysaccharides, which boost the immune system.

2	sticks celery
8	mushrooms
1	onion
3 oz	tahini
2 oz	flaxseed, ground
1 tsp	miso
4 tbsp	water

Roughly chop the celery, mushrooms, and onion, put them in the food processor, and process until they're completely mixed together. Then add the tahini and flaxseeds and process again. Lastly, add miso and water, and process once more, until you have a thick paste. On dehydrator trays, shape into burgers about one-half inch thick, and dehydrate for seven hours.

PER BURGER	
Calories	163
Fat	13.8 g
Carbohydrate	4.5 g
Fiber	4.0 g

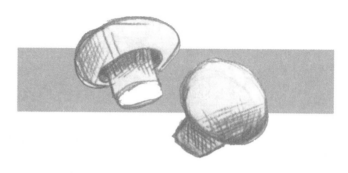

Nut Loaf

This is terrific with Tahini and Miso Gravy (page 51), Eat Your Greens (page 72), and Cauliflower Cheese (page 76). Unfortunately, I've yet to find an adequate raw substitute for roasted potatoes to serve with a traditional Sunday "roast!"

Yield: Serves four

To make nut cutlets, follow the exact same recipe, but shape into burgers instead.

4 oz	almonds
4 oz	walnuts
1 1/2	carrots
2	sticks celery
1	onion
1–2 oz	fresh herbs
1 oz	dried tomatoes
2 oz	flaxseed, ground
2 tbsp	Braggs Liquid Aminos (page 15)
1 tsp	miso

PER SERVING

Calories	542
Fat	44.8 g
Carbohydrate	17.8 g
Fiber	9.6 g

Contains at least 25% of the RDA for: Iron, Vitamins B2, B6, Folate, Vitamins C, A and E

Soak the almonds and walnuts in water for eight hours. When they've finished soaking, drain and grind them as finely as possible in the food processor. Next, roughly chop the carrot, celery, onion, and herbs, put them in the food processor with the nuts and dried tomatoes, and process until there are no large lumps or pieces left. Then add the flaxseed, Braggs, and miso, and process once more until smooth. On a dehydrator tray, shape into a loaf shape about one-inch high and dehydrate for four hours. When done slice and serve.

Sunflower Sausages

Yield: Makes about ten sausages

You can make this mixture into burgers, if you prefer. Pumpkin sausages are marvelous too—just replace the sunflower seeds with ground pumpkin seeds. If you don't have a dehydrator, these work well lightly fried in a pan.

My sons often have these for dinner—they taste far better than a lot of the processed vegetarian sausages you find in the shops.

1 1/2	carrots
6 1/2 oz	cabbage
4 oz	sunflower seeds, ground
2 tbsp	flaxseed, ground
1/2	onion
2 tbsp	nutritional yeast flakes
1 tbsp	tamari

Roughly chop the carrots and cabbage, put all the ingredients in the food processor, and break down to a thick paste. Shape into sausages about one inch by three inches by rolling between the palms of your hands. Dehydrate for four hours.

PER SAUSAGE

Calories	107
Fat	7.2 g
Carbohydrate	6.3 g
Fiber	2.8 g

Contains at least 25% of the RDA for: Folate and Vitamin E

Yield: Serves two

A lot of these recipes demand a high powered blender like a Vita-Mix to work. If your blender is not very strong, try adding the liquid ingredients first and then adding the solid ingredients gradually, with the blender running. Make sure that the mixture keeps turning over. If this doesn't work, you can either add a little water (which makes for a sloppier end product), or use the food processor instead, although the result will be more granular in texture.

Creamy Calcium Vegetables

You can also make this recipe with tofu instead of the almonds. Tofu isn't a raw food but is very high in calcium.

4 oz	ground almonds
1	avocado
2 tbsp	nutritional yeast flakes
2 tsp	tamari
2 tbsp	nori flakes
2	apples, juiced
2	sticks of celery, juiced
4 oz	leafy greens
6 oz	broccoli
6 oz	cauliflower
4 oz	lettuce
	alfalfa sprouts (page 12)

Put all the ingredients in the blender—apart from the broccoli, cauliflower, lettuce, and alfalfa—and blend to make a smooth creamy sauce. Then chop the broccoli and cauliflower finely, shred the lettuce, and place in a serving bowl. Pour the sauce over the vegetables and garnish with alfalfa.

PER SERVING

Calories	687
Fat	50.6 g
Carbohydrate	26.8 g
Fiber	20.0 g

Contains at least 25% of the RDA for: Iron, Zinc, Calcium, Vitamins B1, B2, B3, B6, Folate, Vitamins C, A and E

Dolmades (Stuffed Vine Leaves)

Yield: Serves two

Vine leaves bought in the shops have been boiled. If you or someone you know has a grape vine growing in the garden, you can pick them fresh off the vine. They have a slightly vinegary taste and are crispier than the cooked version, but very tasty. Rinse and soak them in pure water for a few hours before use.

PER SERVING	
Calories	370
Fat	12.0 g
Carbohydrate	59.6 g
Fiber	7.6 g

Contains at least 25% of the RDA for: Iron, Calcium, Vitamins B1, B3, B6, Folate, Vitamins C, A and E

This is one of those Greek dishes that I used to love cooked, but tastes even better raw. If artichokes aren't in season, use white cabbage, celery, or daikon radish instead.

1/2 packet	vine leaves
1 lb	Jerusalem artichokes
1	large onion
3	cloves garlic
1 tbsp	fresh dill
1 tbsp	fresh parsley
1 tbsp	fresh mint
1 tbsp	fresh oregano
1/2 tsp	ground cinnamon
4	tomatoes
	juice 1 lemon
2 tbsp	extra virgin olive oil
1 tsp	tamari
	freshly ground pepper

Firstly, rinse the vine leaves and set aside. Then chop the artichokes in the food processor until the pieces are the same size as rice grains. Put the artichokes in a bowl, and mix the onions, garlic, and tomatoes in the food processor until they're thoroughly broken down. Next, put all the ingredients in the bowl with the artichokes, and stir with a spoon so that they're thoroughly mixed. Place a teaspoon or two of this mixture in each vine leaf, rolling each leaf tightly, and pack them closely in a serving dish. Finally, put them in the refrigerator and leave to marinate for at least a few hours, preferably overnight.

Sprouted Tabbouleh

The grain quinoa was a staple of the Incas. It contains the amino acid lysine, so it provides a more complete protein than other grains. You need to rinse quinoa before you sprout it, to remove its bitter natural coating.

Yield: Serves two

Tabbouleh is a Lebanese salad of bulghur wheat, tomatoes, and fresh herbs, traditionally served with lettuce leaves. The lettuce leaves can be used to scoop up the tabbouleh to eat. This is my version using sprouted alfalfa and quinoa.

2 oz	alfalfa sprouts (page 12)
5 oz	lettuce, shredded
10 oz	quinoa, sprouted (page 13)
4 tbsp	pitted olives
4	tomatoes, chopped
$2/3$	cucumber, chopped
1	red pepper, chopped
1 oz	fresh mint, chopped
small bunch	flat leaf parsley, chopped
	juice 1 lemon
2 tbsp	extra virgin olive oil
2 tbsp	tamari
2	cloves of garlic, minced
$1/2$	onion, chopped

Make a bed for the tabbouleh with the alfalfa and lettuce. Then toss all the other ingredients together until they are evenly distributed, and arrange over the lettuce. If you've got time, leave in the refrigerator for a few hours to marinate.

PER SERVING

Calories	549
Fat	18.0 g
Carbohydrate	83.6 g
Fiber	8.5 g

Contains at least 25% of the RDA for: Iron, Calcium, Vitamins B1, B2, B3, B6, Folate, Vitamins C, A and E

Ratatouille

If possible, make this recipe in advance, as the flavors will blend and the vegetables will soften.

6	mushrooms
2	zucchinis
2	red peppers
1 portion	Pasta Sauce (page 50)

Slice the vegetables as thinly as possible—use the slicing blade on your food processor if you have one. Or you can make zucchini ribbons using a vegetable peeler: peel the zucchini from top to bottom, and keep peeling until you have used as much of the vegetable as you can; finely chop the remainder. Toss the vegetables in Pasta Sauce, top with Grated "Cheese" (page 52) and serve with a green salad.

Yield: Serves two

A traditional Mediterranean dish, the original cooked version contains eggplant, which unfortunately is inedible raw.

PER SERVING

Calories	383
Fat	19.9 g
Carbohydrate	44.6 g
Fiber	9.5 g

Contains at least 25% of the RDA for: Iron, Vitamins B1, B3, B6, Folate, Vitamins C, A and E

ABOUT EQUIPMENT . . .

Raw food preparation relies heavily on the use of a Champion (or similar) juicer and a dehydrator.
If you are serious about eating raw, they are well worth investing in. However, they are expensive pieces of equipment, and before I had either of them I used to read raw food recipe books and get very frustrated by the amount of recipes that I was precluded from. Consequently, wherever possible I have tried to offer alternative methods when these pieces of equipment are used.

Corn Supreme

If you have a spiral slicer, you can use it on the zucchini and carrots and call this pasta! Spiral slicers are machines that you turn by hand to make ribbons of vegetables.

3	carrots
2	zucchinis
2 cobs	sweetcorns
4 oz	sunflower sprouts (page 13)
1 portion	Pasta Sauce (page 50)

Cut off the tops and tails of the carrots. With a vegetable peeler, peel them from top to bottom. Keep peeling until you have used as much of the carrot as you can, and made lots of beautiful orange ribbons (finely chop the remainder). Now do the same to the zucchinis. Because the ribbons are so thin, raw vegetables peeled in this way are very easy to eat, and it makes a welcome change from chopping and grating. Remove the sweetcorn kernels from the cob by holding the cob upright and slicing downwards between the kernels and the core. Hold it over a bowl or a plate to keep the kernels from spraying everywhere. Lastly, put the carrots, zucchini, corn kernels, and sunflower sprouts in a bowl, and toss with the pasta sauce. Top with Grated "Cheese" (page 52).

Yield: Serves two

Like peas, corn is blanched, or dipped into boiling water before it is frozen. Corn on the cob should be bought as fresh as possible, and eaten on the same day: as soon as it is picked, the sugar in the corn begins to turn to starch, and the corn loses its natural sweetness.

PER SERVING

Calories	586
Fat	22.0 g
Carbohydrate	86.5 g
Fiber	11.6 g

Contains at least 25% of the RDA for: Iron, Vitamins B1, B3, B6, Folate, Vitamins C, A and E

Pizza

Yield: Serves two

How densely you cover your pizza is up to you. However, if you pile on too much sauce and layer it with too many toppings, the base is likely to collapse under the weight. These bases are so yummy, it is best not to drown them.

This dish is time-consuming to prepare, but so worth it. Make a batch of bases in advance, and store them in the refrigerator, ready to use. You can't really make the bases without a dehydrator, but you could buy ready-made ones, and still use a raw sauce and topping.

BASES Makes two 8-inch bases

10 oz	buckwheat, sprouted (page 13)
$^1/_2$ oz	fresh basil
1 oz	dried tomatoes
$^1/_2$	onion
1 tbsp	tamari
4 tbsp	extra virgin olive oil

Put the buckwheat in food processor and process for a couple of minutes until it is completely mashed. Add the basil, tomatoes, and onion, and process again so that all are totally amalgamated. Then add the extra virgin olive oil and tamari, and process once more so that you have a smooth batter. Spread two rounds onto dehydrator sheets, about one-quarter inch thick, and dehydrate for twelve hours.

PER SERVING

Calories	1347
Fat	74.1 g
Carbohydrate	135.2 g
Fiber	24.9 g

Contains at least 25% of the RDA for: Iron, Zinc, Vitamins B1, B2, B3, B6, Folate, Vitamins C, A and E

TOPPING

1 portion	Melted "Cheese" (page 52)
1 portion	Pasta Sauce (page 50)
4–8 oz	vegetables (see below)
1 portion	Grated "Cheese" (page 52)

Spread each base with a thin layer of melted cheese, then a thin layer of Pasta Sauce. Cover with vegetables of your own choice such as thinly sliced mushrooms, pitted and halved olives, sweetcorn kernels, thinly sliced tomato, sunflower sprouts, shredded spinach, broccoli florets, thinly sliced onion, or thinly sliced red pepper. Top with Grated "Cheese." Eat immediately before it goes soggy.

Winter Vegetable Stew

Yield: Serves two

Chard is a relative of the beet, and has a similar taste. It's a terrific source of Vitamin A, C, and iron. It's also known as Swiss chard. Ruby chard has a red tinge to it.

PER SERVING

Calories	656
Fat	26.8 g
Protein	25.3 g
Carbohydrate	83.6 g
Fiber	16.1 g

Contains at least 25% of the RDA for: Iron, Zinc, Calcium, Vitamins B1, B2, B3, B6, Folate, Vitamins C, A and E

Wheat grain, sunflower, sesame, and pumpkin seeds together form a complete protein. This is a very hearty dish to keep you going on those cold winter nights.

SAUCE

1 tbsp	sunflower seeds
1 tbsp	pumpkin seeds
1 tbsp	sesame seeds
1 tbsp	hemp seeds
1 tbsp	flax seeds
1 1/2 oz	wheat sprouts (page 13)
1/2	avocado
4	dates
1	onion
3	tomatoes
2 tbsp	dulse
1 tsp	miso
1/4	red chili
2 oz	fresh herbs
8 fl oz	carrot juice

FILLING

5 oz	broccoli
8 oz	chard
4 oz	sunflower sprouts (page 13)

Grind all the seeds together in a grinder. Then put the ground seeds and all the other sauce ingredients into the blender and blend to a thick purée. Next, chop the broccoli and chard into small bite-sized pieces, and mix them into the sauce with most of the sunflower sprouts—reserve some for garnish. Sprinkle the remaining sprouts over the top and serve.

Yield: Serves two

Sprouts are one of the best sources of protein on a raw vegan diet. Many people's diets are too high in protein. As babies, on the other hand, we do more growing than at any other time in our lives, and yet mother's milk contains less than 2-percent protein.

PER SERVING

Calories	623
Fat	24.9 g
Carbohydrate	86.4 g
Fiber	15.8 g

Contains at least 25% of the RDA for: Iron, Vitamins B1, B2, B3, B6, Folate, Vitamins C, A and E

Sweet and Sour

When I used to cook for my husband, I would sometimes buy cook-in sauces for convenience, and add them to a stir fry. When he started to eat raw foods, I tried simply heating these same sauces and adding raw vegetables to them, but the taste was not the best. So I looked at the ingredients on the jars, and realized how simple it would be to make my own, raw sauces.

SAUCE

6	tomatoes
3	carrots
1	onion
4 oz	dates
2 oz	dried tomatoes
4 tbsp	vinegar
2 tbsp	tamari
4 tbsp	extra virgin olive oil
1 inch	piece fresh ginger
2 cloves	garlic
$1/2$	red chili

FILLING

6	mushrooms
2	red peppers
4 oz	snowpeas
4 leaves	bok choy
2 slices	pineapple
4 oz	lentil sprouts (page 13)

Put all the sauce ingredients into the blender and purée for a couple of minutes to make a thick, smooth sauce. Slice the mushrooms and the pepper finely (use the slicing plate on your food processor if you have one). You can use the snowpeas whole, or chop them into smaller pieces if you prefer. Chop the bok choy into small bite-sized pieces, and dice the pineapple. Put all the ingredients, both filling and sauce, in a bowl, and toss together.

Yield: Serves two

Green beans are sprayed with over sixty pesticides—buy organic ones if you can.

PER SERVING

Calories	523
Fat	26.6 g
Carbohydrate	50.3 g
Fiber	20.6 g

Contains at least 25% of the RDA for: Iron, Calcium, Vitamins B1, B2, B3, B6, Folate, Vitamins C, A and E

Thai Green Curry

For red curry, substitute spinach in soup recipe for one red pepper.

one	red pepper
2 portions	Thai soup (page 29)
6 oz	mung bean sprouts (page 13)
8	mushrooms
6 oz	green beans
10 oz	broccoli
10	baby corn

Slice the mushrooms, green beans, broccoli and baby corn into small bite-sized pieces. Reserve one sliced mushroom, and put the rest of the vegetables in a bowl with the sprouts and soup and mix together. Garnish with the remaining mushroom and serve.

Almond Curry

What makes Asian food special is not so much the way it is cooked but the beautiful blend of flavors they use. I used to think that I could never go completely raw because I would miss take-out too much—now we eat Indian, Thai, or Chinese style whenever we choose!

Yield: Serves two

Frozen peas are blanched before freezing, so are not raw. If you have time, buy peas in the pod and shell them yourself—raw peas are much crunchier and taste quite different.

4 oz	ground almonds
8 fl oz	water
4 oz	spinach
1/2	onion
1 tsp	miso
1 tbsp	garam masala
1/4	red chili
4 oz	chick pea sprouts (page 13)
3	mushrooms, sliced
5 oz	cauliflower, chopped
1/2	stick celery, chopped
2 oz	fresh green peas
2 tbsp	almonds

PER SERVING

Calories	676
Fat	47.0 g
Protein	31.4 g
Carbohydrate	33.6 g
Fiber	13.0 g

Contains at least 25% of the RDA for: Iron, Zinc, Calcium, Vitamins B1, B2, B3, B6, Folate, Vitamins C, A and E

In the blender, process the almonds and water to a milk. With the blender turning, gradually add spinach until it has become a thick green liquid. Add onion, miso, garam masala, and chili and blend again until smooth. Next, slice the mushrooms, cauliflower, and celery into small, bite-sized pieces. In a bowl, mix the sauce with the sprouts, mushrooms, cauliflower, celery, peas, and almonds so they are evenly covered. Serve with a sliced mushroom or a sprig of coriander for garnish.

Coconut Curry

When buying fresh coconut, shake it to hear the liquid inside: the more it has sloshing around, the fresher it is.

Lauric acid, the main fatty acid in coconuts (and mother's milk), has antiviral and antibacterial properties.

PER SERVING

Calories	479
Fat	26.7 g
Carbohydrate	52.5 g
Fiber	6.4 g

Contains at least 25% of the RDA for: Iron, Vitamins B1, B3, B6, Folate, Vitamins C, A and E

Fresh coconut is a vital component of a raw food diet, being the only plant source of saturated fats. However, coconut oil does not increase cholesterol levels like the saturated fats found in animal products. Instead, it is one of the most health-giving oils available, being very similar in its make-up to the fats in mother's milk.

SAUCE

$3^1/_2$ oz	creamed coconut (page 144)
$^1/_2$	avocado
2	dates
3	tomatoes
1	carrot
$^1/_2$	onion
2 tbsp	tamari
1 tbsp	garam masala (page 102)
$^1/_4$	red chili
5 fl oz	water

FILLING

2 oz	sunflower sprouts (page 13)
2 tbsp	raisins
1	stick celery, finely chopped
1	carrot, finely chopped
$^1/_4$	daikon radish, grated
2 oz	cauliflower, finely chopped

Blend the coconut, avocado, dates, tomatoes, carrot, onion, tamari, garam masala, chili, and water, to make a smooth sauce. In a bowl, mix the sauce with the remaining ingredients so they are evenly coated. Garnish with carrot ribbons (page 95).

Yield: Serves two

Garam masala is Indian for "warming spices," and adds heat to a dish without being overly spicy. There are many different variations of garam masala available, usually made with a mixture of black pepper, cumin, chili, fennel, cloves, coriander, cardamom, and nutmeg.

Tomato and Asparagus Curry

Asparagus is a member of the lily family, which also includes onions and garlic. It has been cultivated for more than 2,000 years; the ancient Greeks and Romans ate it, and also used it as a medicine.

SAUCE

6	tomatoes
4 tbsp	dried tomatoes
2	sticks of celery
2	carrots
2 tbsp	tamari
4 tbsp	extra virgin olive oil
I	onion
2 tbsp	garam masala
$1/2$	red chili

FILLING

2	carrots, sliced
12	asparagus spears, sliced
6	mushrooms, sliced
4 oz	spinach, shredded
4 oz	lentil sprouts (page 13)
4 tbsp	cashews

PER SERVING

Calories	595
Fat	39.9 g
Carbohydrate	62.2 g
Fiber	16.4 g

Contains at least 25% of the RDA for: Iron, Zinc, Calcium, Vitamins B1, B2, B3, B6, Folate, Vitamins C, A and E

To make the sauce, put the tomatoes, dried tomatoes, celery, carrot, tamari, extra virgin olive oil, onion, garam masala, and chili in the blender. Blend for a couple of minutes until you have a thick smooth sauce. With a vegetable peeler, peel the carrot from top to bottom to make carrot ribbons. Keep peeling until you have used as much of the carrot as you can (finely chop the remainder). Next, slice the asparagus and mushroom into small bite-sized pieces and shred the spinach into small strips by hand. In a bowl, mix the vegetables, sprouts, and cashews into the sauce so the ingredients are evenly covered. Serve garnished with lentil sprouts.

7. Spreads and Puddings

Banana Split

Apple Sandwich

Dates and Tahini

Fruit Salad

Tropical Fruit Pudding

Pear Pudding

Applesauce

Wheatberry Pudding

Avocado Pudding

Mango Sorbet

Banana Ice Cream

Yield: Serves one

Charles Darwin proposed that bananas were man's perfect food. They come in a disposable, biodegradable wrapping that changes color to indicate ripeness. They are shaped to fit snugly in our hands, and contain every nutrient the body needs.

PER SERVING	
Calories	494
Fat	20.5 g
Carbohydrate	69.5 g
Fiber	5.1 g

Contains at least 25% of the RDA for: Irons, Vitamins B1, B3, B6, Folate, Vitamins C and E

Yield: Serves one

I use Thompson raisins rather than standard Muscatel raisins, unless I am mashing them up. Lexias are made from a different variety of grape, and are plumper and juicier.

PER SERVING	
Calories	147
Fat	8.1 g
Carbohydrate	15.3 g
Fiber	3.1g

Banana Split

I had a long phase of eating this for lunch every day. It takes two minutes to prepare, makes the humble banana more interesting, and really hits the spot.

2	bananas
1 tbsp	Nut Butter—cashew or tahini are good (page 34)
1 tbsp	raisins
1 tbsp	seeds such as sunflower and pumpkin

Peel the bananas and slice in half lengthwise. Spread each inside edge with Nut Butter and then cover with dried fruit and seeds. Sandwich the two halves together, and serve.

Apple Sandwich

A fruitarian sandwich!

1	apple
1 tbsp	Nut Butter (page 34)
topping of choice	e.g. sliced grapes, dates, sliced kiwi, berries, raisins

Slice the apple crossways through the core into one-quarter inch slices, so you get circular pieces with beautiful star patterns in the center. Spread each slice on one side with the Nut Butter of your choice. Top with thinly sliced fruits, and eat as is, or sandwich another piece of apple on top.

Yield: Serves 2

Date stones can be grown into houseplants— just plant the stone vertically in compost, and keep it in a warm place until shoots appear.

PER SERVING

Calories	46
Fat	1.5 g
Carbohydrate	7.8 g
Fiber	0.6 g

Yield: Serves two

Some good combinations are: guava, kiwi, and strawberry; mango, papaya, and strawberry; and pineapple and mango. In the autumn, try buying different varieties of apples, and mixing them together.

PER SERVING

Calories	330
Fat	8.1 g
Carbohydrate	62.9 g
Fiber	8.0g

Contains at least 25% of the RDA for: Vitamin B6 and Vitamin C

Dates and Tahini

This may be simple, but it can't be beaten for taste. It is my favorite comfort food. Very sweet and rich, it makes a good chocolate substitute.

4	Medjool dates
2 tsp	Rapunzel white tahini

Remove the stones from the dates and replace with half a teaspoon of tahini.

Fruit Salad

Another recipe that shouldn't be overlooked because of its simplicity. I usually have a fruit meal for lunch, and there are so many permutations of fruit salad, I never tire of it.

6	pieces fresh fruit
1	apple, grated
2	bananas, thinly sliced
2 tbsp	raisins
	dressing of your choice

Chop your favorite fruits into tiny pieces and, in a bowl, mix together with the apple, banana, and raisins. For a plain salad, sprinkle with lemon juice and grated coconut; for a richer dessert, cover with Carob Sauce (page 145) or Cashew Cream (page 146). Or you can try Banana Ice Cream (page 111), or live yogurt.

Yield: Serves two

Papaya contains the
enzyme papain, which
aids digestion.

PER SERVING

Calories	426
Fat	28.0 g
Carbohydrate	41.0 g
Fiber	11.4 g

Contains at least 25% of the
RDA for: Vitamins B2, B6,
Vitamins C, A and E

Yield: Serves two

Ripen unready pears by
putting them in a
brown paper bag on
the window sill. This
works with most fruits.

PER SERVING

Calories	231
Fat	0.9 g
Carbohydrate	55.7 g
Fiber	7.2 g

Contains at least 25% of the
RDA for: Vitamin C

Tropical Fruit Pudding

*Tropical fruits taste best when ripe and freshly picked. This pudding
contains those tropical fruits that are most widely available. It makes
a rich, exotic dessert, appropriate for special occasions.*

2	avocados
1	banana
1	guava
1	mango
$^1/_2$	papaya

Roughly chop all the ingredients, put them in the food
processor, and process to a smooth creamy purée. Top with
grated coconut.

Pear Pudding

*You can serve this as is, or alternatively blend for a puréed pudding.
You can substitute any fruit for the pears—guavas work
particularly well.*

4	pears, chopped
4 tbsp	raisins
4 tbsp	live yogurt
2 tsp	cinnamon
	juice 1 lemon

Put all the ingredients in a bowl and toss together.

Yield: Serves two

PER SERVING	
Calories	283
Fat	0.5 g
Carbohydrate	71.2 g
Fiber	6.2 g
Contains at least 25% of the RDA for: Vitamin C	

Yield: Serves two

There are over 500 varieties of mango, which is known as the apple of the tropics and is a quality source of Vitamins A and C.

PER SERVING	
Calories	442
Fat	1.9 g
Carbohydrate	103.3 g
Fiber	11.0 g
Contains at least 25% of the RDA for: Iron, Vitamins B1, B3, B6, Vitamins C, A and E	

Applesauce

More comfort food.

2 oz	raisins
4 oz	dates or prunes
1 lb	apples, chopped
1 tsp	cinnamon

Put the dried fruit through the Champion juicer with the blank plate on. Then push the apple through the Champion. Add cinnamon, mix all the ingredients together with a spoon, and push through the Champion again. If you don't have a Champion, you can use a food processor instead. Mash the dried fruit until it becomes a homogenized mass—this will take a couple of minutes. Remove from the food processor, and purée the apple until it is completely broken down. Then add the dried fruit and cinnamon back in and process until all the ingredients are blended together.

Wheatberry Pudding

A satisfying pudding. You need to use overripe mango, or it won't blend properly.

6 oz	wheat sprouts (page 13)
2	large mango
4	dates

Roughly chop the mango. Put everything in the blender, and process for a few minutes until it forms a thick purée, making sure no individual wheat sprouts are discernible.

The name "avocado" comes from "ahuacatl," the Aztec word for testical, probably due to the fruit's shape, and because it was thought to be an aphrodisiac.

PER SERVING

Calories	314
Fat	14.3 g
Carbohydrate	45.7 g
Fiber	7.4 g

Contains at least 25% of the RDA for: Vitamin B6, Vitamins C, A and E

PER SERVING

Calories	171
Fat	0.6 g
Carbohydrate	42.3 g
Fiber	7.8 g

Contains at least 25% of the RDA for: Vitamins C, A and E

Avocado Pudding

People seldom think of putting avocados in sweet dishes, but the results are sublime. Avocados are actually neutral, neither sweet nor savory, and when added to fruit make a positively divine pudding.

1	avocado
2	bananas
1–2 pieces	fresh fruit

Roughly chop all the ingredients. Put everything in the food processor and process to a smooth creamy purée.

VARIATIONS

MANGO one large mango, one-half lemon.

COCONUT one apple, one tablespoon raisins, one tablespoon grated coconut.

PEACH AND RED CURRANT one large peach, two tablespoons red currants.

BLACKBERRY AND APPLE one apple, two tablespoons blackberries.

CAROB (*my favorite—a truly ambrosial pudding*) four ounces fresh dates (if using dried, soak for a few hours to soften), one tablespoon carob powder.

Mango Sorbet

Luscious sorbet, free from any sugar or artificial additives

2	mangoes

Peel and slice mangoes, place in a plastic bag and freeze for twenty-four hours. When you're ready to serve it, push the mango through the Champion with the blank plate on, or break it down in the food processor to make a smooth purée.

Yield: Serves two

Many fruits sold in supermarkets are picked unripe, to make it easier to transport and store them. Fruit that has not been given a chance to fully ripen is not as flavorful as fruit that has naturally matured, and will be lacking in vital phytonutrients.

PER SERVING	
Calories	190
Fat	0.6 g
Carbohydrate	46.4 g
Fiber	2.2 g

Contains at least 25% of the RDA for: Vitamins B6 and Vitamins C

Banana Ice Cream

This is my all-time favorite dessert. It's simple to make and an exquisite fat-free alternative to dairy ice cream.

4	bananas

Peel the bananas, break into chunks, and place in a plastic bag. Freeze for twenty-four hours—I have a permanent supply on hand in the freezer. When you are ready to serve the ice cream, remove the chunks from the freezer and put them in the food processor. It takes a few minutes for them to break down—when the ice cream is smooth and creamy it is ready. If you have a Champion, feed them through with the blank plate on for a whipped style result!

VARIATIONS

Add when blending (per single serving):

VANILLA one tablespoon tahini, one teaspoon vanilla extract.

CAROB one tablespoon carob powder, one tablespoon almond butter (page 34).

MINT CHOCOLATE CHIP one teaspoon peppermint extract and four squares plain chocolate or carob, grated.

FRUIT AND NUT one tablespoon chopped, dried fruit, one tablespoon chopped nuts.

BERRY just a handful of berries adds a strong flavor. Try strawberries, blackberries, blueberries.

PEACH one peach and one tablespoon tahini.

8. Cakes and Tarts

Fridge Cake

Crumble Cake

Nut and Banana "Cheesecake"

Apple Crumble

Carrot Cake

Fruit Tart

Ice Cream Cake

"Chocolate" Torte

Christmas Pudding

Christmas Cake

Mincemeat Tart

Fridge Cake

Yield: Makes twenty-five squares

I believe the version of this that you find in wholefood stores and cafes is raw apart from the rolled oats.

This recipe makes a lot, but it keeps well—although it never seems to last long in our house!

CAKE

8 oz	dates (dried rather than fresh)
8 oz	sultanas
4 oz	oat groats, soaked overnight
8 oz	almonds, ground
8 oz	raisins
I oz	carob powder
I tbsp	grain coffee
4 tbsp	molasses
2 oz	grated coconut
2 tsp	mixed spice

ICING

8 oz	tahini
$2^1/_2$ fl oz	apple concentrate
I oz	carob powder

PER SQUARE

Calories	254
Fat	13.0 g
Carbohydrate	30.3 g
Fiber	2.9 g

Contains at least 25% of the RDA for: Vitamin E

Break down the dates and sultanas in the food processor, until they form a homogenized mass. Set aside. Next, put the oats in the food processor, and process until they are mashed completely, with no individual grains discernible. Add the dried fruit back into the food processor along with the almonds, and process until all ingredients are evenly mixed, resulting in a thick, sticky mass. Transfer this to a mixing bowl, and add the rest of the ingredients by hand, stirring with a wooden spoon until thoroughly mixed. Then press it into a nine-and-a-half-inch square tray.

To make the icing, put the tahini and apple concentrate in a bowl and stir with a spoon. Add the carob powder gradually. When it is completely mixed in, spread the icing over the top of the fridge cake. Leave it in a refrigerator for a few hours to harden, then slice it into squares (five up by five down).

Crumble Cake

If you don't have a dehydrator, leave this cake in the oven at the lowest temperature possible, or in a warm place such as an airing cupboard.

CRUMBLE

4 oz	almonds
5 oz	walnuts
4 oz	oat groats, soaked overnight
$2^1/_2$ fl oz	apple concentrate

FRUIT

5 oz	dates or dried apricots
5 oz	apple
1 tsp	cinnamon

Make the crumble and fruit mixtures as detailed in the apple crumble recipe (page 118). Divide the crumble into two equal halves, and press one-half onto a dehydrator sheet.

Spread the fruit mixture over the first layer of crumble, and press a second layer of crumble over the top. Dehydrate for about four hours. When it's done, cut it into sixteen squares.

Yield: Makes sixteen squares

Walnuts have been shown to lower cholesterol levels.

PER SERVING

Calories	169
Fat	11.5 g
Carbohydrate	13.0 g
Fiber	1.7 g

Nut and Banana "Cheesecake"

Psyllium husks are found in drug stores and health food stores, and are usually used as a digestive aid. When added to liquids, the psyllium absorbs the liquid and swells up to form a jelly-like substance. In raw food preparation, this is a way of helping ingredients to solidify without heating them.

This is a basic cake crust that can be used in any raw dish as a replacement for the standard pastry case. It makes a moderately thick crust, which will line the sides and base of the tin. Personally, I prefer a thinner crust which just lines the base, so I often use just four ounces each of almonds and dates. If, on the other hand, you like a really thick crust, use eight ounces of each.

BASE

6 oz	almonds, soaked 8–12 hours
6 oz	dried dates
2 tsp	cinnamon

FILLING

7 oz	cashews, soaked 8–12 hours
4	bananas, roughly chopped
	juice 2 lemons
2 tbsp	apple concentrate
1 tsp	vanilla extract
4 fl oz	apple juice
2 tbsp	powdered psyllium husks

TOPPING

3–6 oz	fresh fruits such as berries, peach slices

In the food processor, grind the almonds as fully as possible. Add the dates and cinnamon, and mix until they have formed one solid mass. You may need to add a drop or two of water to make it stick; no more or it will go soggy. Use this mixture to line the base and sides of a nine-inch cake tin.

Put the cashews, bananas, lemon juice, apple concentrate, and vanilla extract in the blender, adding apple juice gradually—use as little as possible, just enough to make it turn. You will probably not need the full four fluid ounces. Add the psyllium gradually, while the blender is turning. Psyllium starts to set straight away, so as soon as it is mixed in, pour the cashew mix over the base and spread it out evenly, smoothing the top over. Leave to set in the refrigerator for at least a few hours. Top with whatever fresh fruit is in season. Alternatively, top with Carob and Banana Spread (page 146).

PER SERVING

Calories	439
Fat	26.7 g
Carbohydrate	40.0 g
Fiber	4.8 g

Contains at least 25% of the RDA for: Iron, Vitamin B6, Folate, Vitamins C and E

Hippocrates, the Greek philosopher, said "Let food be your medicine and medicine your food."

Apple Crumble

Yield: Serves eight

Apple concentrate is not raw. If you prefer, you can replace it with unpasteurized honey, which is. However, do not serve unpasteurized raw honey to children.

Apple crumble is about as traditional as it gets. It has always been one of my favorite desserts, and I was determined I wasn't going to miss out on it just because I was on a raw diet.

CRUMBLE

4 oz	almonds
5 oz	walnuts
4 oz	oat groats, soaked 8–12 hours
2 ¹/₂ fl oz	apple concentrate

FILLING

4 oz	raisins
2 lb	apple
I tbsp	cinnamon

PER SERVING

Calories	416
Fat	23.2 g
Carbohydrate	45.5 g
Fiber	5.4 g

Contains at least 25% of the RDA for: Vitamin E

To make the crumble, break down the almonds and walnuts in the food processor until they are in evenly sized pieces, about the size of rice grains. Add the oat groats, and process until the oat groats are about the same size. Lastly, add the apple concentrate and process briefly, so that you have a thick, lumpy mass, the same sort of consistency as traditional crumble. Set aside.

If you have a Champion, put the raisins through it, then the apple, then add cinnamon and mix in with a spoon. Otherwise mix all the filling ingredients together in a food processor until you have a purée. Line a nine-inch serving dish with the apple and cover with crumble. Serve with Cashew Cream (page 146) or Banana Ice Cream (page 111).

Yield: Serves eight

In Roman times, carrots were yellow and purple. The modern orange carrot was developed in the fifteenth century. However, purple carrots are now making something of a comeback and are available in some selected supermarkets. Try asking for them if you can't find them in stock.

When I started to buy organic herbs and spices it was a revelation—the tastes are more delicate and subtle, and bring out the flavors in a dish rather than over-power them.

PER SERVING

Calories	541
Fat	38.3 g
Carbohydrate	41.2 g
Fiber	5.9 g

Contains at least 25% of the RDA for: Iron, Vitamins B1, B6, Folate, Vitamin A

Carrot Cake

If you can get it, use organic cinnamon. The flavor is far superior. It took me a long while to realize that it was worth paying extra for all organic ingredients, not just the basics.

6	large carrots
10 oz	walnuts
3 oz	fresh coconut
$^1/_2$ inch	piece fresh ginger
4 oz	dates
2 oz	raisins
2 oz	dried apricots
1 tbsp	cinnamon
$^1/_2$ tsp	grated nutmeg

ICING

4 oz	cashews, soaked for 8–12 hours
6 $^1/_2$ oz	raisins, soaked for 1–2 hours
1 tsp	vanilla extract
4 fl oz	water

Juice the carrots. Drink the juice or save for later. Remove the pulp from the juicer and set aside. If you have a Champion, put the blank plate on and process the walnuts, then the coconut, ginger, and finally the dried fruit. Otherwise, put these ingredients in the food processor and break down for a couple of minutes until you have a homogenized mass. Then transfer the mix to a large bowl, and, using a wooden spoon, stir in the carrot pulp and the spices until they are thoroughly and evenly blended. Press into a nine-inch cake tin.

To make the icing, put the ingredients in the blender, adding as little water as possible to make the icing thick (start with two fluid ounces, and add the rest gradually).

Spread the icing over the carrot cake, and leave in the refrigerator for at least a few hours. The cake will keep for about a week—the flavors improve with age.

Yield: Serves six

The top five most nutritious fruits are guava, watermelon, grapefruit, kiwi, and papaya.

PER SERVING

Calories	374
Fat	20.5 g
Carbohydrate	40.2 g
Fiber	6.2 g

Contains at least 25% of the RDA for: Vitamins C and E

Fruit Tart

This is one of my favorites, and a raw food classic. Very simple to make, and with so many variations, you will never tire of it. It serves as a welcome introduction to raw foods for cynical guests.

CRUST

6 oz	almonds, soaked 8–12 hours
6 oz	dried dates
2 tsp	ground cinnamon

FILLING

4–6	pieces fresh fruit (see below)
1	large banana
2 tbsp	dates
2 tbsp	tahini
	juice 1 lemon

In the food processor, grind the almonds as fully as possible. Add the dates and cinnamon, and mix until they have formed one solid mass. You may need to add a drop or two of water to make it stick; no more or it will go soggy. Use this mixture to line the base and sides of a nine inch cake tin.

Slice your fresh fruit and arrange decoratively over the base. Try mango, kiwi, papaya, peach, strawberry, plain old apple, or any mixture that you fancy—like mixed berries for a summer tart, or mango, papaya, and guava for a tropical tart.

Blend the remaining ingredients in the food processor until they form a thick sauce with no lumps left. Pour the sauce over the fruit, spreading it evenly into all the nooks and crannies. Serve immediately—and try not to eat it all at once! For a richer, creamier tart, you may like to double the amount of sauce, so that the fruit is smothered in it rather than just lightly coated.

Yield: Serves eight

China is now the world's biggest fruit producer, followed by Brazil and the USA.

PER SERVING

Calories	272
Fat	11.3 g
Carbohydrate	38.8 g
Fiber	3.2 g

Contains at least 25% of the RDA for: Vitamin E

Ice Cream Cake

For variations, see Banana Ice Cream (page 111). This is a lovely one to make in the summer, as it keeps indefinitely. I break chunks off, and snack on it straight from the freezer. I also keep it on hand to serve surprise guests.

CRUST

4 oz	almonds, soaked 8–12 hours
4 oz	dried dates
2 tsp	cinnamon

TOPPING

8	bananas, broken into pieces and frozen at least 24 hours beforehand
1 tbsp	apple concentrate
2 tbsp	tahini
1 tbsp	raisins
1 tbsp	sunflower seed sprouts (page 13)

In the food processor, grind the almonds as fully as possible. Add the dates and cinnamon, and mix until they have formed one solid mass. You may need to add a drop or two of water to make it stick; no more or it will go soggy. Use this mixture to line the base and sides of a nine-inch cake tin.

If you have a Champion, put the bananas through with the blank plate on; if not, the food processor will do (it will take a few minutes for them to break down this way—when the ice cream is smooth and creamy it is ready). Add the remaining ingredients to the bananas and mix them in with a wooden spoon. Spoon the ice cream onto the base and serve immediately. Store the leftovers in the freezer. You can eat it straight from the freezer, or defrost in the refrigerator for ten to fifteen minutes first, for a softer cake.

"Chocolate" Torte

This has to be tasted to be believed; it makes an amazing deep chocolatey dessert. Serve this to your guests and see if anyone can guess the secret ingredient—they will not believe you when you tell them.

CRUST

6$^1/_2$ oz	fresh coconut (or desiccated if fresh is unavailable)
4 oz	ground cashews
1	banana

FILLING

10 oz	plain black olives, pitted
14$^1/_2$ oz	dates
1 oz	carob powder
1 tbsp	grain coffee
1 tbsp	ground cinnamon
1 tbsp	vanilla extract
6 fl oz	water
2 tbsp	powdered psyllium husks

Yield: Serves twelve

Like avocados, black olives have a surprisingly neutral flavor, and work well with fruit. It's vital that you use plain, pitted black olives that have been soaked in brine rather than marinated in any oils or herbs that will flavor the olives.

PER SERVING

Calories	218
Fat	14.2 g
Carbohydrate	19.6 g
Fiber	3.3 g

To make the crust, chop the coconut in the food processor until it is completely broken down. Add the ground cashews and process until they are mixed together. Put the banana in a chunk at a time, just enough to hold it all together. Use to line the base of a nine-inch cake tin.

To make the filling, break down the olives in the food processor. Add the dates and process until a paste is formed. Then add the carob, grain coffee, cinnamon, and vanilla, and blend thoroughly. Keep the machine running, and pour in the water. Finally, add the psyllium gradually, while the machine is on. After a minute, turn the machine off, and immediately spoon the mixture onto the coconut base before the psyllium starts to set. Spread out evenly with a knife, and leave in the refrigerator for a few hours to firm.

christmas Pudding

Both Christmas Cake and Christmas Pudding contain mostly dried fruit, so it is easy to replicate raw versions.

Yield: Makes eight small puddings

The following three recipes are raw food variations of three delicious traditional English desserts.

8 oz	dried figs
4 oz	almonds
3 oz	sprouted wheat (page 13)
2 oz	dates
2 oz	dried apricots
2 oz	raisins
2 oz	currants
1 tbsp	molasses
2 tbsp	apple concentrate
1	orange, juiced
1 tsp	miso
1 tbsp	ground cinnamon
1 tsp	ground ginger
pinch	ground nutmeg
pinch	ground cloves

PER SERVING

Calories	279
Fat	9.8 g
Carbohydrate	44.0 g
Fiber	4.6 g

Contains at least 25% of the RDA for: Iron and Vitamin E

If you have a Champion juicer, put the blank plate on. Push through the almonds, then the sprouted wheat, then the figs, dates, apricots, raisins, and currants. If you're using a food processor, grind the nuts and transfer them to a mixing bowl. Break down the figs until they form a homogenized mass, and transfer them to the bowl. Then break down the dates, apricots, raisins, currants, and sprouted wheat together, until they form a thick paste with no discernible individual ingredients, and transfer them to the bowl as well. Next, add in the remaining ingredients and mix thoroughly with a wooden spoon until all the ingredients are completely blended. On a dehydrator tray, shape into eight small Christmas puddings, and dehydrate for four hours. Serve warm, straight from the dehydrator (if you don't have a dehydrator, you can eat them just as they are).

christmas cake

This takes some time to prepare, and is very rich, but will allow you to feel suitably decadent when you sit down to Christmas dinner.

This is adapted from a recipe that was in the first Fresh magazine I ever received. I have made it every year since, and I always think that it is such a big cake, I will never eat it all. Of course, there is never any left by January.

CAKE

5 oz	walnuts
4 oz	almonds
3 oz	sprouted wheat (page 13)
8 oz	dried figs
2 oz	dates
2 oz	dried apricots
2 oz	raisins
2 oz	currants
1 tbsp	molasses
1	orange, juiced
1 tsp	miso
1 tbsp	cinnamon
1 tsp	ginger
pinch	grated nutmeg
pinch	ground cloves

MARZIPAN

6 1/2 oz	almond butter (page 34)
3 tbsp	apple concentrate
1 tbsp	vanilla extract

ICING

6 1/2 oz	creamed coconut
4 oz	dates
1 tbsp	apple concentrate

PER SERVING

Calories	453
Fat	30.2 g
Carbohydrate	37.3 g
Fiber	4.9 g

Contains at least 25% of the RDA for: Iron and Vitamin E

The cake works best if you have a Champion juicer. With the blank plate on, put through the walnuts and almonds, then the sprouted wheat, then the figs, dates, apricots, raisins, and currants. If you're using a food processor, grind the nuts and transfer them to a mixing bowl. Break down the figs until they form a homogenized mass, and transfer them to the bowl. Then break down the dates, apricots, raisins, currants, and sprouted wheat until they form a thick paste with no discernible individual ingredients, and transfer them to the bowl as well.

Add the remaining ingredients and mix thoroughly with a wooden spoon until the ingredients are completely amalgamated. Line a deep seven-and-a-half-inch cake tin with greaseproof paper and fill it with the cake mixture. Leave it in the refrigerator for a few hours to harden.

To make the marzipan, add the vanilla to the almonds and mix. Add the apple concentrate gradually until a thick paste is formed. Turn the cake out from the tin, and spread a thin layer of the marzipan over the top and sides of the cake. It is better to have some marzipan left over than to make it too thick.

To make the icing, push the coconut through the Champion with the blank plate on, followed by the dates (or put both in the food processor and process until they form a homogenized mass). Add the apple concentrate and stir in with a wooden spoon. Ice the cake while the coconut is still soft, using just enough to cover the marzipan layer—again, don't use it all unless you have to (the remainder can be rolled into balls and eaten as sweets).

Leave overnight to set. This cake will keep for several weeks, if given a chance.

Mincemeat Tart

If you are trying to eat raw at Christmas time, it is very hard not to be tempted unless you have your own treats to succumb to instead.

CRUST

6 oz	almonds, soaked 8–12 hours
6 oz	dried dates
2 tsp	cinnamon

MINCEMEAT

1	orange
1	lemon
12 oz	grated apple
4 oz	raisins
4 oz	sultanas
4 oz	currants
2 oz	dates, chopped
1 tbsp	ground cinnamon
1 tsp	ground ginger
pinch	ground nutmeg
pinch	ground cloves
2 tbsp	flax oil
1 tbsp	apple concentrate
1 tbsp	molasses
1 tsp	miso

Use organic, unwaxed lemons and oranges. Non-organic fruits are covered in an inedible wax that makes them more shiny and so supposedly more desirable to the consumer.

In the food processor, grind the almonds as fully as possible. Add the dates and cinnamon, and mix until they have formed one solid mass. You may need to add a drop or two of water to make it stick; no more or it will go soggy. Use this mixture to line the base and sides of a nine-inch cake tin.

Juice the lemon and the orange, and grate the rind. Mix all the mincemeat ingredients together in a large bowl. Use a wooden spoon, and make sure everything is evenly mixed. Press the mincemeat onto the crust. If you can bear not to start in straight away, leave it in the refrigerator for at least a few hours to allow the flavors to mingle, and serve with Cashew Cream (page 146) or Banana Ice Cream (page 111). It keeps well in the refrigerator for a week or two (if given the chance).

9. Breads, Crackers, and Cookies

Essene Bread

Carrot and Raisin Bread

Banana Loaf

Molasses Cookies

Lemon Cookies

Date Cookies

Figgy Cookies

Banana Date Cookies

Coconut Cookies

Mango Cookies

Ginger Snaps

Flapjack Bars

ESSene Bread

The seeds and wheat grain in this loaf together form a complete protein. This is not the sort of bread you can easily slice and spread or make a sandwich with. Much better to break chunks off, dab on a little tahini, and just eat it as it is.

The Essene bread usually sold in healthfood stores is not raw, but as it is made from sprouted wheat, it is still a healthier choice than conventional bread.

People who have problems with cooked wheat products are unlikely to encounter the same problems with sprouted wheat. This is because when the grain is sprouted, the enzymes break down the heavy, complex starches into simple sugars, proteins into amino acids, and fats into fatty acids. Therefore, they are said to be predigested.

5 oz	wheat, sprouted (page 13)
4 oz	dates
4 oz	raisins
2 tbsp	sesame seeds
2 tbsp	sunflower seeds
2 tbsp	pumpkin seeds
2 tsp	cinnamon

Put all the ingredients in the food processor. Break down as much as possible, so there are no individual ingredients discernible, just one thick mass. If you have a Champion, put this mix through with the blank plate on—it will make it much more of a loaf. Shape it into a loaf about two inches high. Dehydrate for approximately eighteen hours.

PER SLICE (10 SLICES)	
Calories	135
Fat	4.8 g
Protein	3.5 g
Carbohydrate	20.6 g
Fiber	1.2 g

**Yield: Makes about
a one pound loaf**

PER SLICE (10 SLICES)	
Calories	59
Fat	0.3 g
Protein	1.0 g
Carbohydrate	13.7 g
Fiber	0.6 g

Carrot and Raisin Bread

A lovely, sweet loaf. Serve with carob and banana spread (page 146).

6 oz	sprouted wheat (page 13)
3	carrots
8 oz	raisins
2 tsp	cinnamon
pinch	ground cloves
pinch	grated nutmeg

Put the wheat sprouts, carrots, and raisins through the Champion with the blank screen on. Mix in the spices with a spoon. Shape it into a loaf about two inches high. Dehydrate for twelve hours.

**Yield: Makes about
a one pound loaf**

If your bananas are overripe, or you add too many, this will be too runny to make a loaf—just make it into banana cookies instead by dehydrating the mixture for about fifteen hours!

PER SLICE (10 SLICES)	
Calories	81
Fat	1.2 g
Protein	2.0 g
Carbohydrate	16.7 g
Fiber	0.7 g

Banana Loaf

This is a very moist loaf, more like cake than bread.

12 oz	sprouted wheat (page 13)
4	bananas
4 oz	raisins
2 tbsp	sesame seeds

Put all the ingredients through the blender with the blank screen on. On a dehydrator tray, shape into a loaf about two inches high. Sprinkle with sesame seeds, and dehydrate for around eighteen hours.

Molasses Cookies

This is a gorgeous, golden-brown cookie—a batch never lasts more than a few days in our house.

10 oz	buckwheat, sprouted (page 13)
4 fl oz	extra virgin olive oil
2 tbsp	apple concentrate
2 tbsp	molasses
2 tsp	cinnamon
2 oz	raisins
2 tbsp	sunflower seeds

Put the buckwheat in the food processor, and process for a couple of minutes until it becomes a thick mash. Add the extra virgin olive oil, apple concentrate, molasses, and cinnamon, and blend until you have a thick batter. Next, stir in the raisins and sunflower seeds with a spoon. Make into thin cookie shapes around three to four inches in diameter, and dehydrate for about fifteen hours.

Yield: Makes about twenty-five cookies

When buying extra virgin olive oil, look for labels that state that the oil is from the "first cold-pressing" only. These oils are the technically raw. To confuse matters, many oils which are labeled simply "cold-pressed" actually undergo high temperatures during the manufacturing processes.

PER COOKIE

Calories	86
Fat	5.3 g
Carbohydrate	8.7 g
Fiber	0.3 g

Lemon Cookies

A refreshing cookie. The sweetness of the raisins counteracts the tartness of the lemon.

10 oz	buckwheat, sprouted (page 13)
4 fl oz	extra virgin olive oil
4 fl oz	apple concentrate
1	lemon (unwaxed)
2 oz	raisins

Put the buckwheat in the food processor, and process for a couple of minutes until it becomes a mash. Add the flesh of the lemon, carefully removing any seeds, and half of the peel, grated, and blend in. Next add the extra virgin olive oil and apple concentrate, and process to a thick batter. Stir the raisins into the batter with a spoon. On dehydrator trays, make into thin cookie shapes around three to four inches in diameter, and dehydrate for about fifteen hours.

Yield: Makes about thirty cookies

Extra virgin olive oil is the only oil that is suitable for human consumption in its natural state; all other oils need to go through some kind of treatment to make them edible. Olives are a fruit, so extra virgin olive oil is really just fruit juice.

PER COOKIE	
Calories	75
Fat	4.6 g
Carbohydrate	7.6 g
Fiber	0.7 g

**Yield: Makes about
fifteen crackers**

The essential fatty acids
in flaxseed are very
good for the brain. If
you are not eating fish,
it is important that you
try and eat flaxseed (or
hemp seed, which is
also a rich source of
fatty acids) every day.

PER CRACKER	
Calories	56
Fat	1.5 g
Carbohydrate	9.4 g
Fiber	1.4 g

**Yield: Makes about
fifteen crackers**

Figs were one of man's
first foods, and the
most mentioned fruit in
the Bible. They contain
more fiber than any
other fruit or vegetable.

PER CRACKER	
Calories	48
Fat	1.4 g
Carbohydrate	7.6 g
Fiber	1.2 g

Date Crackers

*These crackers are even more delicious with a spread, such as Toffee
Spread (page 145), or Carob and Banana Spread (page 146).*

6 oz	sprouted wheat (page 13)
2 oz	flaxseed, ground
4 oz	dates
1 tsp	cinnamon
8 fl oz	water

Put all the ingredients into the blender and purée until you have
a smooth batter. On dehydrator sheets, make into thin cracker
shapes around three to four inches in diameter, and dehydrate
for twelve hours.

Figgy Crackers

*These crackers are perfect for taking out with you, as they are not
as crumbly as some of the other recipes, and taste delightful just
as they are.*

1	lemon
4 oz	oat groats, soaked overnight
2 tbsp	flaxseed, ground
4 oz	dried figs
8 fl oz	water

Peel the lemon, remove the seeds, use all the flesh pulp and
juice, and discard the rest. Put the lemon flesh and the
remaining ingredients into the blender and purée to a smooth
batter. On dehydrator sheets, make into thin cracker shapes
around three to four inches in diameter, and dehydrate for
about twelve hours.

Banana Date Cookies

These cookies were inspired by Jo's Cake (page 161). The cake is so popular, I thought I would see if a raw version is as delectable —it is!

inspired by Jo's Cake (page 161).

Yield: Makes about twenty-five cookies

Bananas are the most popular fruit in the world. They contain elements of almost all we need nutritionally, including all eight of the essential amino acids.

3	bananas
4 fl oz	extra virgin olive oil
6 $^1/_2$ oz	oats, soaked overnight
6 oz	dates
1 tsp	cinnamon
2 tbsp	flaxseeds, ground

Mash the bananas in the food processor until there are no lumps left. Blend the extra virgin olive oil, bananas, and oats in the blender until the oats are completely broken down and the mixture is a smooth batter. Next, mash the dates in the food processor until they are a homogenized mass. Gradually add the oat mix to the dates in the food processor, and process until it is thoroughly amalgamated. Finally, add in the cinnamon and flaxseeds and process again, until you have a thick gloopy mass. Place dessert spoons of the mixture onto the dehydrating sheet and dehydrate for eighteen to twenty-four hours. Store in the refrigerator.

PER COOKIE	
Calories	98
Fat	5.6 g
Carbohydrate	10.9 g
Fiber	1.4 g

Coconut Cookies

These are divine!

4		bananas
6 $^1/_2$ oz		fresh coconut
4 oz		cashews, ground
4 oz		raisins

Roughly chop the bananas and coconut. Put the bananas in food processor, and process until they are liquefied. Add the coconut, and mix until it is very finely chopped. Then add the cashews, and process briefly until they are evenly mixed in. Lastly, stir in the raisins with a spoon. Put dollops of the mixture onto dehydrator trays, and dehydrate for around eighteen hours.

VARIATIONS

Replace banana with eight ounces apple and one tablespoon vanilla extract. Dehydrate twelve hours only.

Replace banana with one large mango.

Yield: Makes about twenty cookies

Raw food preparation is marvelous for children to participate in. Most recipes have very simple methods that children can be fully involved in; what's more, they can taste the fruits of their labors immediately (and no need to worry about indigestion if they eat too much of the mixture).

PER COOKIE

Calories	107
Fat	6.7 g
Carbohydrate	10.5 g
Fiber	1.3 g

Mango Cookies

These are deliciously sweet, fruity cookies.

2	large mangoes
6 oz	sprouted wheat (page 13)
2 oz	raisins
4 oz	apple

Remove the flesh of the mango from the peel and the stone. Put the flesh in the blender with the remaining ingredients and blend until you have a smooth batter. You may need to add a little water or apple juice to help it turn over; not too much or your mixture will be too gloopy. On dehydrator trays, shape into cookie shapes and dehydrate for eighteen hours.

Ginger Snaps

This is a crunchy, stimulating cookies. Add more ginger if you are a real fan.

10 oz	buckwheat, sprouted (page 13)
4 fl oz	extra virgin olive oil
2 oz	flaxseed, ground
4 fl oz	apple concentrate
3 oz	freshly grated ginger

Put the buckwheat in the food processor, and process for a couple of minutes until you have a thick mash. Then add the remaining ingredients and blend to make a thick batter. On dehydrator trays, make into thin cookie shapes around three to four inches in diameter, and dehydrate for about fifteen hours.

Flapjack Bars

Yield: Makes eighteen bars

Apple and raisin flapjacks are my favorite, but you can substitute whatever nut or fruit you like, or even add two table-spoons carob powder for a carob flapjack.

A firm favorite in our family, and unbelievably like the cooked version. If I had known how to make things like this when I first got interested in raw foods, it would have made the transition a lot easier.

8 oz	oat groats, soaked overnight
4 fl oz	extra virgin olive oil
4 fl oz	apple concentrate
2 tsp	cinnamon
2 oz	raisins
2 oz	apple, chopped finely

Put the oats in the food processor. Process for a few minutes, making sure that the grains are completely broken down into a paste. Add the extra virgin olive oil, apple concentrate, and cinnamon, and process to a smooth batter. Lastly, stir in the raisins and apple with a spoon. Spread into a square about one-half inch high on dehydrator sheet. Dehydrate for about eighteen hours. When cooled cut into eighteen bars.

PER COOKIE	
Calories	140
Fat	7.6 g
Carbohydrate	17.1 g
Fiber	1.1 g

10. Sweet Things

Sweets

Apricot Balls

Coconut Kisses

Halva

White "Chocolate"

Calcium Candies

Selenium Sweets

Christmas Sweets

Coconut Ice

Toffee Spread

Carob Sauce

Carob and Banana Spread

Cashew Cream

Sweets

When I make sweets, I use measuring cups to make life easy. The basic recipe is two cups dried fruit to one cup nuts or seeds. They are best made in a Champion juicer, but if you don't have one, a food processor will do fine. Use dried dates, unless otherwise stated.

These sweets are so popular, especially with children. Whenever I make them for other people, they invariably rave about them and ask for the recipe. They are incredibly simple to make, and you can use whatever combination of nuts and dried fruits that you choose; listed here are some of my favorites. Decorated with sesame seeds or grated coconut, they make lovely homemade gifts. Each recipe makes about twenty-five sweets (depending on how big you roll the balls and how much you eat while you're making it). One friend says she melts a bar of plain organic chocolate into the recipe to make wonderful truffles, but I wouldn't know about that!

CHAMPION METHOD

With the blank plate on, feed the nuts or ground seeds through first, then the dried fruit. Add any extra ingredients to the bowl, and mix together with a wooden spoon.

When it's become a single solid mass, take walnut-sized balls of the mixture and roll between the palms of your hands to form balls. Store in the refrigerator.

FOOD PROCESSOR METHOD

Grind the nuts or seeds in a grinder, or use Nut Butter (page 34).

Break down the dried fruit in the food processor until it forms one homogenous mass. By hand, break the mass into smaller pieces, and then add the nuts or seeds and any extra ingredients. Turn the food processor on again, and keep it turning until it forms a mass again. This will take a few minutes; be patient. You may need to add a few drops of water to get it to hold together, but be careful: any more than a few drops and it will become too sticky. When it's become a single solid mass, take walnut-sized balls of the mixture and roll between the palms of your hands to form balls. Store in the refrigerator.

Yield: Approximately twenty-five sweets

PER SWEET	
Calories	65
Fat	4.2 g
Protein	1.2 g
Carbohydrate	5.9 g
Fiber	0.7 g

Apricot Balls

Both apricots and raisins are high in iron, which is especially important for women.

5 oz	walnuts
4 oz	dried apricots
4 oz	raisins
1 tsp	cinnamon

Prepare ingredients as described on page 140.

Yield: Approximately twenty-five sweets

PER SWEET	
Calories	35
Fat	1.5 g
Protein	0.3 g
Carbohydrate	5.4 g
Fiber	0.5 g

Coconut Kisses

Fresh dates and coconut go really well together and make a charming snack just as they are.

3 1/2 oz	fresh coconut
4 oz	fresh dates
4 oz	raisins
1 tbsp	carob powder

Prepare ingredients as described on page 140.

Yield: Approximately twenty-five sweets

PER SWEET	
Calories	88
Fat	5.9 g
Protein	2.1 g
Carbohydrate	7.1 g
Fiber	1.1 g

Yield: Approximately twenty-five sweets

PER SWEET	
Calories	77
Fat	4.8 g
Protein	2.0 g
Carbohydrate	6.8 g
Fiber	0.5 g

Yield: Approximately twenty-five sweets

PER SWEET	
Calories	53
Fat	3.0 g
Protein	1.4 g
Carbohydrate	5.6 g
Fiber	1.1 g

Halva

When I make these, I find it really hard not to eat them all as I make them. If I want to have any left after the family has got to them, I have to triple or quadruple the recipe!

8 oz	tahini
4 oz	raisins
4 oz	dates
1 tsp	vanilla extract

Prepare ingredients as described on page 140.

White Chocolate

Although they may not look anything like their namesake, they have a similarly luxurious, creamy taste.

8 oz	cashews
4 oz	dates
4 oz	raisins

Prepare ingredients as described on page 140.

Calcium Candies

Both almonds and figs are very high in calcium, so these are especially suitable to give to children.

4 oz	almonds
8 oz	dried figs
1 tbsp	lemon juice

Prepare ingredients as described on page 140.

Yield: Approximately twenty-five sweets

PER SWEET	
Calories	62
Fat	3.4 g
Protein	1.0 g
Carbohydrate	7.2 g
Fiber	0.5 g

Selenium Sweets

Brazil nuts are the highest natural source of selenium. Good for the boys!

4 oz	brazil nuts
4 oz	raisins
4 oz	dates or dried apricots
I tbsp	carob powder

Prepare ingredients as described on page 140.

Yield: Approximately twenty-five sweets

PER SWEET	
Calories	57
Fat	2.9 g
Protein	1.4 g
Carbohydrate	6.7 g
Fiber	0.8 g

christmas Sweets

Like miniature Christmas puddings.

4 oz	almonds
4 oz	dried figs
4 oz	raisins
I tsp	cinnamon
	juice $1/2$ orange
pinch	ground cloves
pinch	grated nutmeg

Prepare ingredients as described on page 140.

Coconut Ice

Yield: Makes about thirty squares

The jelly coconut is an unripe coconut and very popular in Asia. If you ever get a chance to try one, hack the top off, drink the juice, and scoop out the soft, jelly-like meat out with a spoon. It is absolutely exquisite.

PER SQUARE	
Calories	41
Fat	3.3 g
Protein	0.5 g
Carbohydrate	2.4 g
Fiber	0.2 g

A very popular sweet. If you're feeling lazy, leave out the beet and make a plain white sweet. If you can't get fresh beet juice, best to omit it rather than use artificial coloring.

13 oz	creamed coconut
8 oz	dates
1	beet, peeled and juiced
2 tbsp	grated coconut

If you have a Champion juicer, you can make your own creamed coconut. Push fresh coconut through the Champion with the blank screen on. Then push it through again, this time with the juicing screen on. This "juice" is your coconut cream, and is absolutely heavenly, but doesn't keep for more than a few days, and must be stored in the refrigerator.

Put the dates through the Champion with the blank screen on. Mix the dates and coconut together with a wooden spoon until they have formed a solid mass. Divide the mixture into two halves. Add the beet juice to one-half of the mixture a few drops at a time, until it is a nice pink color. Press the white half into a twenty-three-centimeter (nine-inch) tray, and then press the pink half on top. Sprinkle grated coconut evenly over the top, and press in.

Leave to set in the refrigerator for a few hours. When it is hard, chop into squares.

If you don't have a Champion, use store-bought creamed coconut (which is not strictly raw). Either leave it in a warm place to melt or break it into chunks. Put it in the food processor, processing until it turns into a runny mass with no lumps. Break down the dates in the food processor separately, until they form a homogenized mass. Then mix the dates and coconut together in the food processor until you get a smooth paste.

Molasses is a by-product of sugar cane manufacturing, and not a raw food, but is a valuable source of iron, calcium, and vitamin B.

PER 15 g TABLESPOON	
Calories	49
Fat	1.4 g
Protein	0.8 g
Carbohydrate	8.7 g
Fiber	1.1 g

Carob powder is made from the pods of the fruit, not the seeds. If you are lucky enough to find carob pods they make wonderful snacks: you chew on the pod and spit out the seeds.

PER 15 g TABLESPOON	
Calories	21
Fat	0.8 g
Protein	0.5 g
Carbohydrate	3.1 g
Fiber	0.2 g

Toffee Spread

This makes an incredibly thick, sticky spread, very intense in flavor and crammed with nutrients. Spread sparingly on crackers or Essene bread.

5 oz	molasses
2 oz	flaxseed, ground
1 tbsp	carob powder
$^1/_2$ tsp	vanilla extract

With a wooden spoon, combine the molasses and flaxseed, then add the carob and vanilla. Keeps indefinitely.

Carob Sauce

Pour over chopped fruit, or have a raw fondue and dip slices of fruit into the carob sauce.

1	banana
2 tbsp	carob powder
1 tbsp	tahini
	water

Break the banana into chunks and put all the ingredients in the blender or food processor. Blend until you get a smooth creamy sauce. Add water according to how thick you want the sauce: a little for a fruit dip, more for a fruit dressing.

Carob and Banana Spread

This goes wonderfully on crackers and loaves.

2	bananas
2 oz	almond butter (page 34)
2 tbsp	carob powder

Break down the bananas in the food processor until they are liquefied. Add the almonds, then carob powder. Process to a thick paste.

Cashew Cream

For a lighter, fluffier cream, soak the cashews overnight before using.

4 oz	cashews
2 oz	dates
1 tsp	vanilla extract
	water

Blend all the ingredients. Start off with half a cup of water, and then add a tablespoon at a time until you reach the desired consistency. Half a cup makes a stiff cream, one cup for a pouring cream.

Yield: About a half cup

Carob is popular as an alternative to cocoa not just because it is caffeine-free, but is lower in fat, high in protein, and contains many vitamins and minerals including calcium.

PER 15 g TABLESPOON	
Calories	32
Fat	1.8 g
Protein	0.9 g
Carbohydrate	3.2 g
Fiber	0.3 g

Yield: About a half cup

This is marvelous with any pudding, such as Fruit Salad (page 107) or Apple Tart (page 120), or you can use it as icing for a cake.

PER 15 g TABLESPOON	
Calories	42
Fat	3.2 g
Protein	1.2 g
Carbohydrate	2.3 g
Fiber	0.3 g

11. Drinks

Rejuvelac Wine

Mango Lassi

JUICES

Carrot and Apple

Beet

Cucumber

Sunshine Juice

Carrot and Orange

Apple

Orange and Apple

Peach

SMOOTHIES

Basic Recipe

Heaven in a Glass

Carob Shake

Guava I

Guava II

MILKS

Nut Milk

Banana Milk

RejuVelac Wine

Rejuvelac is the name given to the soak water of wheat grain. It is full of nutrients and enzymes. Anne Wigmore, founder of the Hippocrates Health Institute, was a great believer in the restorative powers of fermented foods such as rejuvelac and sauerkraut.

2 tbsp	wheat grain
2 tbsp	dried fruit
I tbsp	seeds or nuts
$^1/_2$	cinnamon stick
$^1/_2$ inch	piece fresh ginger
3	fresh cloves

Place all the ingredients in a large jar, and fill with about one and one-quarter pints of pure water. Leave for twelve hours. At the end of this time, place the contents of the jar in the blender and blend until completely liquefied.
Then transfer back to the jar, and leave for a further twenty-four hours.
Finally, strain and serve.

Yield: Serves two

Next time you soak wheat for sprouting, don't throw the water away. You can drink it straight, or if the taste is too much for you, you can mix it with other drinks. Many raw foodists use rejuvelac in place of pure water in recipes such as soups and pâtés. If you mix rejuvelac with ground seeds and leave it to ferment for a day or two, it makes a seed cheese which you can use as an accompaniment to salads or as a spread for crackers.

PER SERVING

Calories	67
Fat	2.1 g
Carbohydrate	10.8 g
Fiber	1.05 g

Contains at least 25% of the RDA for: Vitamin E

Mango Lassi

Yield: Serves two

Lassi is a traditional Indian drink served with spicy food, to help cool the palate. It is usually made with yogurt, and if you prefer, you can substitute the cashews, lemon, and water with a half pint live soy yogurt, although cashews and lemon blended together do have a distinctly yogurty flavor. Serve with Onion Bhajis (page 66), Spicy Carrot and Apple Salad (page 70), and Curried Spinach (page 67) for a complete Indian meal.

You can use either ice or water, or a mixture of both, depending how chilled you want your lassi. It is very difficult to get good quality mangoes. They are usually picked unripe and stored at very low temperatures, which makes them last the journey, but then instead of ripening properly, they go straight to overripe. Mangoes are a heavily sprayed crop, so go for organic wherever possible.

1	small mango
1	lemon
2 oz	ground cashews
2	sprigs mint
4	dates
1/2 pint	water or ice cubes

Peel and chop the mango and lemon, being careful to remove the lemon pips. Stone the dates, and remove the mint leaves from the stems. Put everything into the blender. Blend until smooth.

Juices

Juices are the best way to get a blast of nutrients without taxing your digestive system. Freshly made juice is incomparable to the shop-bought version, and once you've started making your own, you won't ever want to go back to the packaged stuff. Orange juice, for instance, loses 70 percent of its nutritional value within an hour of being squeezed. There are many quality books on the market about the benefits of juicing and suggestions for recipes. I've included here a few of my favorites, but the permutations are endless. Just one rule: for ease of digestion, don't mix fruits and vegetables, carrots and apples being the only exceptions. Apples work particularly well in adding sweetness to some of the more bitter vegetable juices.

Remove any unwanted stems, roots, etc. Peel oranges and beets. Feed all ingredients through the juicer and drink immediately. For best results, if you're using lemon, or any herbs and spices, juice them in the middle of the other ingredients, not first or last, to make sure they get properly juiced.

Carrot and Apple

Yield: About one cup

Very good for the digestion.

3	carrots
I	apple
I	stick celery
$^1/_4$	red chili (optional)

Prepare ingredients as described above.

PER SERVING	
Calories	133
Fat	0.8 g
Carbohydrate	31.1 g
Fiber	7.6 g

Contains at least 25% of the RDA for: Vitamins C and A

Yield: About one cup

PER SERVING	
Calories	110
Fat	0.3 g
Carbohydrate	25.6 g
Fiber	5.0 g

Contains at least 25% of the
RDA for: Folate

Yield: About one cup

PER SERVING	
Calories	76
Fat	0.3 g
Carbohydrate	17.3 g
Fiber	3.4 g

Yield: About one cup

PER SERVING	
Calories	143
Fat	1.0 g
Carbohydrate	31.7 g
Fiber	7.1 g

Contains at least 25% of the
RDA for: Vitamin B6, Folate,
Vitamins C, A and E

Beet

Sweet purple power!

3	small beets
1	apple

Prepare ingredients as described on page 150.

Cucumber

Very refreshing on a summer's day.

1/2	cucumber
1	apple
1	sprig mint

Prepare ingredients as described on page 150.

Sunshine Juice

Grocery stores often sell big bags of peppers for next to nothing, and this is a lovely way to use them up.

1	red pepper
1	yellow pepper
1	apple

Prepare ingredients as described on page 150.

Yield: About one cup

PER SERVING	
Calories	192
Fat	0.9 g
Carbohydrate	43.8 g
Fiber	10.5 g

Contains at least 25% of the RDA for: Calcium, Vitamin B6, Folate, Vitamins C, A and E

Yield: About one cup

PER SERVING	
Calories	178
Fat	0.5 g
Carbohydrate	44.1 g
Fiber	6.5 g

Contains at least 25% of the RDA for: Vitamin C

Yield: About one cup

PER SERVING	
Calories	235
Fat	0.6 g
Carbohydrate	56.2 g
Fiber	9.8 g

Contains at least 25% of the RDA for: Vitamins B1, B6, Folate, Vitamin C

Carrot and Orange

Blend in an avocado, and you've got a soup!

3	carrots
2	oranges

Prepare ingredients as described on page 150.

Apple

Experiment with different varieties of apple. You'll be amazed at the difference in flavor.

3	apples
$^1/_4$	lemon (unwaxed, with peel on)
$^1/_2$ inch	piece fresh ginger

Prepare ingredients as described on page 150.

Orange and Apple

I have this for breakfast most days, usually with a good dose of ginger, some Klamath Lake blue-green algae, and a teaspoon of flax oil.

2	apples
2	oranges
$^1/_4$	lemon (unwaxed, with peel on)

Prepare ingredients as described on page 150.

Peach

Juicing the lemon peel as well as the flesh adds an extra zest to your juice.

2	apples
1	peach
$^1/_4$	lemon (unwaxed, with peel on)

Prepare ingredients as described on page 150.

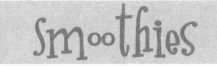

Smoothies

Smoothies have become increasingly popular in recent years, and although there are some fine makes in the shops, you can't beat doing it yourself. A meal in a glass, they serve well as breakfast or lunch when you're in a hurry, or make an easily digestible dessert.

Basic Recipe

3	pieces of fruit, juiced
$^1/_2$	banana (frozen for a cold smoothie)
1	piece fresh fruit

Put all the ingredients in the blender and purée until smooth. For an extra energy lift, add some Aloe Vera or Klamath Lake blue-green algae. For a beneficial dose of essential fatty acids, add one to two teaspoons of flax oil.

Yield: About one cup

PER SERVING	
Calories	461
Fat	4.3 g
Carbohydrate	103.2 g
Fiber	17.4 g

Contains at least 25% of the RDA for: Calcium, Vitamins B1, B2, B6, Folate, Vitamins C, A and E

Heaven in a Glass

This is my all-time favorite smoothie.

I	medium mango, peeled and cubed
3	oranges, juiced
$^1/_4$	lemon (unwaxed, with peel on)
I tsp	tahini
I	date
$^1/_2$	frozen banana

Prepare ingredients as described on page 153.

Yield: About one cup

PER SERVING	
Calories	349
Fat	10.2 g
Carbohydrate	61.8 g
Fiber	8.2 g

Contains at least 25% of the RDA for: Iron, Calcium, Vitamins C and E

Carob Shake

There are many different makes of grain coffee on the market, all much the same: a blend of barley, rye, chicory, and figs, which tastes not dissimilar to coffee. I often add a little when I am using carob in a recipe to deepen the flavor and give it more of a dark chocolate taste.

3	apples, juiced
2 tbsp	dates
I tbsp	tahini
I tbsp	carob powder
I tsp	cinnamon
I tsp	grain coffee

Prepare ingredients as described on page 153.

GuaVa I

Guavas are possibly my favorite fruit. They bring a wonderful tropical aroma to my kitchen, and add an exotic touch to any smoothie.

Yield: About one cup

PER SERVING	
Calories	236
Fat	0.9 g
Carbohydrate	57.7 g
Fiber	9.3 g

Contains at least 25% of the RDA for: Vitamin B6 and Vitamin C

3	apples, juiced
1	guava, roughly chopped
$1/_2$	banana
$1/_4$	lemon (unwaxed, with peel on)

Prepare ingredients as described on page 153.

GuaVa II

Guavas are a wonderful source of Vitamin C, Vitamin B1, Vitamin B2, niacin, and phosphorus.

Yield: About one cup

PER SERVING	
Calories	217
Fat	2.0 g
Carbohydrate	49.0 g
Fiber	11.0 g

Contains at least 25% of the RDA for: Vitamins C and E

2	pears, juiced
1	apple, juiced
1	guava, roughly chopped
2 tbsp	soy yogurt
$1/_4$	lemon (unwaxed, with peel on)

Prepare ingredients as described on page 153.

You can make milk with virtually any nut, seed, or vegetable when you blend it with water, but these are two of the tastiest and most nutritious options. Sesame milk is also popular, but a little bitter.

Milks

There are many different alternatives to cow's milk, such as rice milk, oat milk, and of course soy milk. In some wholefood stores, you can even find raw goat's milk. Although they may be a healthier option than cow's milk, they are still heavily processed and denatured. It takes no time at all to make your own milk, and it's also relatively inexpensive.

Yield: About one cup

PER SERVING	
Calories	184
Fat	16.7 g
Carbohydrate	2.1 g
Fiber	2.2 g

Contains at least 25% of the RDA for: Vitamin E

Nut Milk

2 tbsp	almond butter (page 34)
8 fl oz	water

Blend for a few minutes. Strain and serve. Add date, banana, or apple concentrate if sweetner is desired. Alternatively, soak two tablespoons of almonds in eight fluid ounces of water overnight. In the morning, blend, strain, and serve as a delicious breakfast milk.

Yield: About one cup

PER SERVING	
Calories	95
Fat	0.3 g
Carbohydrate	23.2 g
Fiber	1.1 g

Banana Milk

1	banana
8 fl oz	water

Blend for a few minutes until the banana is liquefied.

12. Not Really Raw

Potato Salad

The Best "Fries"

Nana's Chutney

Jo's Cake

Potato Salad

Yield: Serves two

None of the recipes in this section are raw, but I wanted to include them as healthier alternatives to the usual fare. They're all sugar-free, wheat-free and dairy-free.

As potatoes raise the blood sugar level, it's not sensible to eat them in large quantities. So whenever you serve them it's a good idea to substitute sweet potatoes for at least half the quantity of white potatoes.

12 oz	white potatoes
12 oz	sweet potatoes
2 tbsp	hemp seeds
4 tbsp	chopped spring onion
2 tbsp	fresh parsley, finely chopped
2–4 tbsp	mayonnaise (depending on thickness) (page 47)
	salt and pepper, to taste

Chop both types of potato into cubes about one-inch square. Bring to the boil, and simmer for eight minutes. Drain and leave to cool, then transfer to a bowl, and with a spoon, toss with the remaining ingredients.

PER SERVING

Calories	491
Fat	17.7 g
Carbohydrate	78.0 g
Fiber	12.0 g

Contains at least 25% of the RDA for: Iron, Vitamins B1, B6, Folate, Vitamins C, A and E

The Best "Fries"

Yield: Serves two

It was years before I stopped craving fries. This is what I would have, and it is a relatively healthy option, as well as being far yummier than any oven or fast food fries.

12 oz	potatoes
12 oz	sweet potatoes
2 tbsp	extra virgin olive oil
2 tbsp	tamari

Other vegetables that make delectable fries are celeriac, beet, and squash. Parsnips are good, but you need to steam or blanch them for a few minutes first or they will be too woody.

Chop potatoes into fingers about a half-inch by four inches. Place on baking tray and pour over just enough extra virgin olive oil and tamari to coat them.

Bake 425°F for fifteen minutes. Take the fries out and stir them, if necessary adding some more extra virgin olive oil to prevent sticking. Cook for another fifteen minutes. Serve with a large green salad.

PER SERVING

Calories	405
Fat	11.9 g
Carbohydrate	72.5 g
Fiber	6.8 g

Contains at least 25% of the RDA for: Vitamins B1, B6, Folate, Vitamins C, A and E

Nana's Chutney

This spicy side-dish is easy to make, and goes well with just about any salad. Much better than a store-bought jar full of sugar and salt.

Yield: About one and a half cups

This is adapted from a recipe my grandmother gave me. Although it is cooked, it includes so many of my favorite ingredients I couldn't leave it out.

6 fl oz	apple cider vinegar
3 tbsp	molasses
4 oz	dates, chopped
2	cloves garlic, finely chopped
1/4 inch	piece fresh ginger, finely chopped
1/2	red chili, finely chopped
2 tbsp	raisins
1 tsp	miso

Put vinegar and molasses in pan and bring to boil. Add dates, garlic, ginger, and chili, and simmer gently for fifteen minutes, stirring occasionally to prevent sticking. Next, add the raisins and simmer for a further five minutes, stirring occasionally. Stir in the miso at the end of cooking. Leave to cool and transfer to a jar. Store in the refrigerator; keeps indefinitely.

PER 15 g TEASPOON	
Calories	19
Fat	0.0 g
Protein	0.2 g
Carbohydrate	4.8 g
Fiber	0.2 g

Yield: Serves eight

Jo gave me this recipe a few years ago, and I have used it ever since whenever a birthday cake is called for. It has a gorgeous, light taste and is quick and easy to make, and someone always asks for the recipe.

PER SERVING

Calories	564
Fat	39.9 g
Carbohydrate	40.0 g
Fiber	5.8 g

Contains at least 25% of the RDA for: Iron, Calcium, Vitamins B1, B6, Folate

Jo's Cake

This is the best cake ever—no nasties, and still so scrumptious. It's the only really stunning wheat-free, sugar-free, dairy-free cake I've ever come across.

2 oz	rolled oats
6 oz	dates
3	bananas
4 fl oz	extra virgin olive oil
3 oz	soy flour
3 oz	rice flour
3 tsp	bicarbonate of soda

ICING

10 oz	tahini
2$^1/_2$ fl oz	apple concentrate
1 oz	carob powder
	water

Break the oats down into flour in a food processor, remove, and set aside. Break down dates in food processor until they form a homogenized mass. Then add bananas, extra virgin olive oil, and oats to the dates, and process again to make a smooth batter. Put in the rest of ingredients and process once more until they are completely mixed in. Spoon into a greased seven-and-a-half-inch cake tin and bake at 325°F for sixty to seventy minutes. Turn out, and ice when cool.

To make the icing, put all the ingredients in a bowl, and stir together with a spoon, adding a little water at a time until it is the right consistency—thin enough to spread, but not too runny.

ABOUT THE AUTHOR

Kate Wood lives in Brighton, England with her husband and three sons. The whole family eats mostly raw foods. Kate has been on a high raw diet since the early nineties; Chris, since 2000; and the children have been brought up this way. The boys love their food, and are a shining example of the benefits of the diet. Kate has a wealth of writing experience, including editing *Fresh* magazine, the UK raw foods publication, and being assistant editor of *Juno*, a wholistic parenting magazine. She is also a popular speaker, admired for her down-to-earth, natural approach.

Kate set up the Raw Living company as a response to the increasing demand for raw food products and advice in the UK. Every single item stocked in the shop is used by Kate and her family on a regular basis, so you know they must be good! The company also produces Raw Highs, a unique range of raw energy snack bars and trail mixes, including the best-selling cacao snacks Hi-bar and Hi-trail.

Raw Living opened the first raw shop in the UK in Brighton, where customers are able to buy juices, salads, and sweets from the deli; see the equipment in action; and attend a workshop or lecture. As well as conducting events across the country, Raw Living is involved in organizing raw food festivals, primarily Food of Life and Funky Raw, and running retreats in Ibiza and Lanzarote. The raw foods revolution is sweeping many parts of the world, including North America and the UK, and Raw Living is at the forefront! It is a tremendously exciting time to be part of a thriving and vibrant scene that is contributing so positively to people's lives, and helping to create a better world for us all.

To find out more you can visit www.rawliving.co.uk.

RESOURCES

Groups, Practitioners, and Websites

Here is a list of some of the foremost raw practitioners and organizations in the North America. It is not a comprehensive list, but a selection of those whose approach I recommend. There are many "raw food experts" around nowadays. Before taking anyone's advice, please check out their credentials, find out how long they have really been raw, and how the diet actually works for them.

Most of those mentioned here offer a full package of support, advice, workshops, events, and publications, as well as online shops. Contact them to find out what is going on in the raw food scene in your area. There are plenty of amazing raw food restaurants around the country, as well as regular speaking events, workshops, and pot lucks.

Alissa Cohen

The astounding Alissa offers raw chef training, books, dvds, an online shop and more.

148 Chiquita St
Laguna Beach, California 92651
1 (888) 900-2529 / 978-985-7217

www.alissacohen.com

Hippocrates Health Institute

The home of wheatgrass, founded by Anne Wigmore and Viktoras Kulvinskas, now run by the eminent Brian Clements and his wife Anna Marie. They are internationally renowned for their program for people with life-threatening illnesses. Visitors learn about a variety of healing methods, the core approach being the living foods diet of green salads, juice and wheatgrass. They also run the Hippocrates health educator program for those wishing to train in living foods, and offer retreats at their luxury facilities for those just looking for a healthy getaway.

1443 Palmdale Court
West Palm Beach, FL 33411 USA
561-471-8876

www.hippocratesinst.com

Living Nutrition

Headed by David Klein, Living Nutrition produces a popular magazine, published twice a year. They are one of the most well-established raw foods organizations around, and promote the Natural Hygiene approach. The website has a huge amount of information and resources.

P.O. Box 256
Sebastopol, CA 95473
(707) 829-0362

www.livingnutrition.com

Nature's First Law

Founded by the unstoppable David Wolfe, Nature's First Law is probably the world's premier raw food organization, with its headquarters and raw food superstore in California. David is often in the media, and holds lectures and retreats around the world. Their website rawfood.com is the world's leading online raw shop, stocking all the unusual and exotic ingredients you can't find anywhere else.

PO Box 900202
San Diego, CA 92190
(800) 205-2350 or 888-RAW-FOOD

www.rawfood.com

Raw Family

The Boutenko family, Victoria, Igor, Sergei, Valya are an inspirational example of an entire family thriving on raw foods. They have published several books, and give lecture tours across the country.

P.O.Box 172
Ashland, Oregon 97520

www.rawfamily.com

Raw Guru

Alex Malinsky does it all! Offers catering, workshops, a comprehensive website and online shop.

RawGuru, INC.

3211 De Leon St. Suite #1
Tampa, Fl. 33609
1-800-577-4RAW

www.rawguru.com

Tree of Life Rejuvenation Center

The retreat center of Dr. Gabriel Cousens, highly respected raw practitioner. Dr Cousens originally trained as an MD, but now approaches health from a wider perspective. Spirituality is an important part of the Tree of Life approach, which encompasses yoga and meditation as part of a raw lifestyle. As well as retreats and the world famous apprenticeship program for raw chefs, they offer an online shop and a café.

686 Harshaw Road
Patagonia, AZ 85624
866-394-2520

www.treeoflife.nu

The Vegetarian Resource Group (VRG)

The Vegetarian Resource Group (VRG) is a wonderful non-profit organization dedicated to educating the public on all aspects of vegetarianism and the interrelated issues of health, nutrition, ecology, ethics, and world hunger. In addition to publishing the Vegetarian Journal, *VRG produces and sells cookbooks, other books, pamphlets, and article reprints.*

P.O. Box 1463, Dept. IN
Baltimore, MD 21203
(410) 366-VEGE (8343)

www.vgr.org

Vital Creations

Chad Sarno is one of the world's premier raw chefs. His website offers recipes and resources as well as details of his catering services.

1-888-276-7170

www.rawchef.org

Equipment

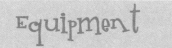

There are a number of products I would like to recommend. My recommendations are based on the performance of these machines as I have used them over the years.

The Champion Juicer

They are a family owned company that manufactures a line of heavy duty juicers that work well with various juicing and grinding techniques. To learn more about their products and where to buy Champion juicers, visit their website.

www.championjuicer.com

The Green Power Juicer

They manufacture a fine line of juice extractors. They are also marketed under the name Green Star. To learn more about their equipment and where to buy Green Power products, visit their website.

www.greenstar.com

Vita-Mix Corporation

They manufacture a fine line of heavy duty blenders and food processors. These machines are capable of liquifying most fruits and vegetables. To learn more about their equipment and where to buy Vita-Mix products, visit their website.

www.vitamix.com

Recommended Reading

There are dozens of raw books on the market to choose from. These are the ones that have inspired me the most.

Naked Chocolate by David Wolfe and Shazzie published by Nature's First Law, 2005.

The recipes in this book were written before the outrageous cacao bean came on the raw food scene, but if you want the lowdown on the healthiest food in the world, check out this book and website at www.naked-chocolate.com.

The Rainbow Green Live Food Cuisine by Dr. Gabriel Cousens published by North Atlantic Books, 2003.

Gabriel Cousens has an amazing amount of knowledge and decades of experience with raw foods. His books are always persuasive and revealing.

Sunfood Diet Success System by David Wolfe published by Maul Brothers Publishing, 3rd edition, 2000.

For inspiration and motivation, this book is a raw bible. Every home should have one.

The Uncook Book by Juliano published by Regan books, 1999.

The original and the most successful raw gourmet recipe book. Juliano is a dynamic raw chef who has a restaurant in California. You can find out more at www.planetraw.com.

Metric Conversion Tables

COMMON LIQUID CONVERSIONS

Measurement	=	Milliliters
1/4 teaspoon	=	1.25 milliliters
1/2 teaspoon	=	2.50 milliliters
3/4 teaspoon	=	3.75 milliliters
1 teaspoon	=	5.00 milliliters
1 1/4 teaspoons	=	6.25 milliliters
1 1/2 teaspoons	=	7.50 milliliters
1 3/4 teaspoons	=	8.75 milliliters
2 teaspoons	=	10.0 milliliters
1 tablespoon	=	15.0 milliliters
2 tablespoons	=	30.0 milliliters

Measurement	=	Liters
1/4 cup	=	0.06 liters
1/2 cup	=	0.12 liters
3/4 cup	=	0.18 liters
1 cup	=	0.24 liters
1 1/4 cups	=	0.30 liters
1 1/2 cups	=	0.36 liters
2 cups	=	0.48 liters
2 1/2 cups	=	0.60 liters
3 cups	=	0.72 liters
3 1/2 cups	=	0.84 liters
4 cups	=	0.96 liters
4 1/2 cups	=	1.08 liters
5 cups	=	1.20 liters
5 1/2 cups	=	1.32 liters

CONVERTING FAHRENHEIT TO CELSIUS

Fahrenheit	=	Celsius
200–205	=	95
220–225	=	105
245–250	=	120
275	=	135
300–305	=	150
325–330	=	165
345–350	=	175
370–375	=	190
400–405	=	205
425–430	=	220
445–450	=	230
470–475	=	245
500	=	260

CONVERSION FORMULAS

LIQUID		
When You Know	Multiply By	To Determine
teaspoons	5.0	milliliters
tablespoons	15.0	milliliters
fluid ounces	30.0	milliliters
cups	0.24	liters
pints	0.47	liters
quarts	0.95	liters

WEIGHT		
When You Know	Multiply By	To Determine
ounces	28.0	grams
pounds	0.45	kilograms

INDEX

GOING WILD IN THE KITCHEN
The Fresh & Sassy Tastes of Vegetarian Cooking

Leslie Cerier

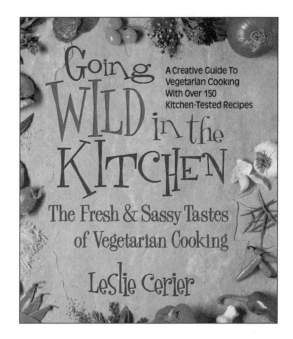

A Creative Guide To Vegetarian Cooking With Over 150 Kitchen-Tested Recipes

As vegetarianism's popularity continues to gain momentum, organic foods are making their way to the forefront of a health-conscious nation. Author and expert chef Leslie Cerier is crazy about the great taste and goodness of organically grown foods. In her latest cookbook, *Going Wild in the Kitchen,* Ms. Cerier shares scores of her favorite recipes that spotlight these fresh, wholesome foods.

Going Wild in the Kitchen is the first comprehensive global vegetarian cookbook to go beyond the standard organic beans, grains, and vegetables. In addition to providing helpful cooking tips and techniques, the book contains over 150 kitchen-tested recipes for healthful, taste-tempting dishes—creative masterpieces that contain such unique ingredients as edible flowers; sea vegetables; and wild mushrooms, berries, and herbs. It encourages the creative side of novice and seasoned cooks alike, prompting them to follow their instincts and "go wild" in the kitchen by adding, changing, or substituting ingredients in existing recipes. To help, a wealth of suggestions is found throughout. A list of organic foods sources completes this user-friendly cookbook.

Going Wild in the Kitchen is both a unique cookbook and a recipe for inspiration. So let yourself go! Excite your palate with this treasure-trove of unique, healthy, and taste-tempting recipe creations.

ABOUT THE AUTHOR

Leslie Cerier is a gourmet organic caterer, cooking instructor, and nutritional expert. She is the author of *The Quick and Easy Organic Gourmet* and coauthor of *Sea Vegetable Celebrations.* Ms. Cerier has published dozens of articles over the past fifteen years focusing on such topics as vegetarian cooking, nutrition, organic gardening, and natural living.

$16.95 US / $25.50 CAN • 240 pages • 7.5 x 9-inch quality paperback • 2-Color • ISBN 0-7570-0091-6

AS YOU LIKE IT COOKBOOK

Imaginative Gourmet Dishes with Exciting Vegetarian Options

Ron Pickarski

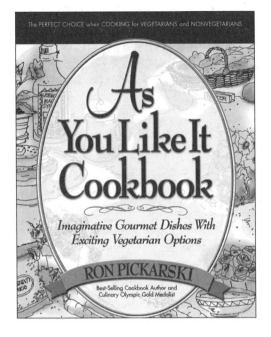

When it comes to food, we certainly like to have it our way. However, catering to individual tastes can pose quite a challenge for the cook. Have you ever prepared a wonderful dish, but because it contained beef or chicken, your daughter-in-law, the vegetarian, wouldn't go near it? To meet the challenge of cooking for vegetarians and non-vegetarians alike, celebrated chef Ron Pickarski has written the *As You Like It Cookbook.*

Designed to help you find the perfect meals for today's contemporary lifestyles, the *As You Like It Cookbook* offers over 175 great-tasting dishes that cater to a broad range of tastes. Many of the easy-to-follow recipes are already vegetarian—and offer ingredient alternatives for meat eaters. Conversely, recipes that include meat, poultry, or fish offer nonmeat ingredient options. Furthermore, if the recipe includes eggs or dairy products, a vegan alternative is given for those who follow a strictly plant-based diet. This book has it all—delicious breakfast favorites, satisfying soups and sandwiches, mouth-watering entrées and side dishes, and delectable desserts.

With one or two simple ingredient substitutions, the *As You Like It Cookbook* will show you how easy it is to transform satisfying meat dishes into delectable meatless fare, and vegetarian dishes into meat-lover's choices. It will guide you in making culinary decisions that result in meals that are gratifying and delicious, and cooked exactly as you (and your family) like them.

ABOUT THE AUTHOR

Ron Pickarski is the first professional vegetarian chef to be certified executive chef by the American Culinary Federation, and is President and Chef/Consultant of Eco-Cuisine, Inc., a food technology consulting service. A recognized expert in the preparation of both traditional and vegetarian cuisine, Mr. Pickarski is also the author of *Eco-Cuisine: An Ecological Approach to Gourmet Vegetarian Cooking.*

$16.95 US / $25.50 CAN • 216 pages • 7.5 x 9-inch quality paperback • Full-Color Photos • ISBN 0-7570-0013-4

**For more information about our books, visit our website at
www.squareonepublishers.com**